T0376091

Advanced Introduction to the Sociology of Peace Processes

Elgar Advanced Introductions are stimulating and thoughtful introductions to major fields in the social sciences, business and law, expertly written by the world's leading scholars. Designed to be accessible yet rigorous, they offer concise and lucid surveys of the substantive and policy issues associated with discrete subject areas.

The aims of the series are two-fold: to pinpoint essential principles of a particular field, and to offer insights that stimulate critical thinking. By distilling the vast and often technical corpus of information on the subject into a concise and meaningful form, the books serve as accessible introductions for undergraduate and graduate students coming to the subject for the first time. Importantly, they also develop well-informed, nuanced critiques of the field that will challenge and extend the understanding of advanced students, scholars and policy-makers.

For a full list of titles in the series please see the back of the book. Recent titles in the series include:

Landmark Criminal Cases
George P. Fletcher

Comparative Legal Methods
Pier Giuseppe Monateri

U.S. Environmental Law
E. Donald Elliott and Daniel C. Esty

Gentrification
Chris Hamnett

Family Policy
Chiara Saraceno

Law and Psychology
Tom R. Tyler

Advertising
Patrick De Pelsmacker

New Institutional Economics
Claude Ménard and Mary M. Shirley

The Sociology of Sport
Eric Anderson and Rory Magrath

The Sociology of Peace Processes
John D. Brewer

Advanced Introduction to

The Sociology of Peace Processes

JOHN D. BREWER

Professor of Post Conflict Studies, Senator George J. Mitchell Institute of Global Peace, Security and Justice, Queen's University Belfast, UK, Honorary Professor Extraordinary, Stellenbosch University, South Africa, and Honorary Professor of Sociology, Warwick University, UK

Elgar Advanced Introductions

Cheltenham, UK • Northampton, MA, USA

© John D. Brewer 2022

All rights reserved. No part of this publication may be reproduced, stored in a retrieval system or transmitted in any form or by any means, electronic, mechanical or photocopying, recording, or otherwise without the prior permission of the publisher.

Published by
Edward Elgar Publishing Limited
The Lypiatts
15 Lansdown Road
Cheltenham
Glos GL50 2JA
UK

Edward Elgar Publishing, Inc.
William Pratt House
9 Dewey Court
Northampton
Massachusetts 01060
USA

A catalogue record for this book
is available from the British Library

Printed on elemental chlorine free (ECF)
recycled paper containing 30% Post-Consumer Waste

ISBN 978 1 83910 738 2 (cased)
ISBN 978 1 83910 740 5 (paperback)
ISBN 978 1 83910 739 9 (eBook)

Printed and bound in the USA

For Caitríona, Bronwen, Gwyn, Fiachra, Russell, Lori, Matilda, Toby, Merryn, Juliet and Theo
My wife, children and grandchildren are my proudest and most enduring accomplishment

Contents

Acknowledgements		ix
1	**Introduction: an autobiography of the book**	**1**
2	**From the sociologies of order and conflict to the sociologies of war and peace**	**4**
	Introduction	4
	The sociology of order	4
	The sociology of conflict	7
	Transcending the two sociologies debate	9
	The sociology of violence and war	13
	The re-enchantment of the social sciences	15
	Conclusion	21
3	**Understanding what peace means sociologically**	**23**
	Introduction	23
	What is peace?	23
	What is a peace process?	30
	Compromise peace processes	35
	Conclusion	42
4	**The sociology of compromise after conflict**	**44**
	Introduction	44
	A sociological approach to compromise	45
	Emotions as performed behaviour	47
	Conclusion	60

viii ADVANCED INTRODUCTION TO THE SOCIOLOGY OF PEACE PROCESSES

5	**The sociology of post-conflict emotions**	**63**
	Introduction	63
	A critique of emotions in transitional justice studies	64
	Towards a sociology of post-conflict emotions	68
	Conclusion	80
6	**The sociology of everyday life peacebuilding**	**82**
	Introduction	82
	What is everyday life?	83
	What is everyday life peacebuilding?	85
	Mundane reasoning and everyday life peacebuilding	86
	Practical reasoning and discordant accounts	97
	Conclusion	98
7	**Notes towards a sociology of personal trauma**	**100**
	Introduction	100
	The sociology of cultural trauma	101
	Notes towards a sociology of personal trauma	106
	Conclusion	118
8	**Conclusion: why the sociology of peace processes matters**	**119**
	Introduction	119
	Summary of the argument	119
References		128
Index		139

Acknowledgements

I wish to thank Stephen Harries, my editor from Edward Elgar Publishers, both for the kind invitation to contribute to this series of Advanced Introductions and his patience in the half-year delay in writing it because of the COVID-19 pandemic. The book is the culmination of a professional life and thus I have developed many debts to friends and colleagues who shared some of my interests. First mention must be the Leverhulme Trust Compromise After Conflict research programme team, especially Bernie Hayes, Francis Teeney, Katrin Dudgeon, Natascha Mueller-Hirth and Shirley Lal Wijesinghe, whose six years together flew past but have left a life-long memory and friendship. I have shared book publications with many co-authors and co-editors down the years. These include, in addition to those mentioned above, Gareth Higgins, Dave Mitchell, Gerard Leavey and, most recently, Azrini Wahidin. I am grateful for this association and their many kindnesses. I owe thanks to mentors when I was young, like Jack Spence from Leicester and the late John Rex from Warwick, and to Chris Jenks and Richard Breen for friendship and support in my later professional life. I have had the value of good friendships during some prolonged research visits abroad, such as the late Fatima Meer, Peter Derman and Pumla Gobodo-Madikizela in South Africa, John Braithwaite and Clifford Shearing in Australia, and Shirley Lal Wijesinghe and Dipthee Silva in Sri Lanka. I wish to thank my colleagues and friends in the Senator George J. Mitchell Institute who provided me such a congenial, warm and encouraging intellectual space in which to work, especially Hastings Donnan, Kieran McEvoy, Gladys Ganiel and Fiona Murphy, with whom I have worked the closest.

I could not mention Queen's without closing with acknowledgement to my dear friend David Livingstone. I am grateful to John Scott, Neil McLaughlin and Azrini Wahidin for their comments on earlier drafts. Thanks to all. Once more, love to my family who have borne the cost of my professional life.

1 Introduction: an autobiography of the book

In 2018 I submitted, anonymously, an article to two of Britain's sociology journals in turn on the topic of the sociology of everyday life peacebuilding. Both declined to send it out to review stating on a preliminary read by editors that its problematic and audience were not sociological. This might be as a result of my failings as the author of course, although a book with the same title was published that year after rigorous peer review (see Brewer et al. 2018). I prefer, naturally, to see it differently. Journal editors and referees are the chief custodians of the boundaries of disciplines, guarding tenaciously what passes for them as normal science. Inter- and cross-disciplinary work has a hard time convincing discipline-based journals of their publishable merits, which is why there is now a plethora of inter-disciplinary journals to cater for such work. As we shift into what elsewhere I have described as a post-disciplinary research environment (Brewer 2013a), custodians of disciplinary boundaries will need to confront the appropriateness of their practices.

I am by identity and inclination a sociologist, now in my fifth decade as a professional sociologist. The discipline made sense of my life (see Brewer 2015a) and gave me a life. Thus, I always preferred to write for my discipline, rather than inter-disciplinary journals, for my intent was to engage sociology with new and innovative topics, demonstrating how it was enriched by new fields. The sociological imagination should not be constrained by what custodians take it to mean. Custodians of disciplinary boundaries engage in disciplinary closure, especially when innovative work does not have a critical mass of people working on it.

This has been my experience with the sociology of peace processes. The psychology of peace is an established sub-field, especially in the United States of America. As is, for example, military anthropology in the USA. They have many adherents working away diligently, assisted by the sheer

1

2   ADVANCED INTRODUCTION TO THE SOCIOLOGY OF PEACE PROCESSES

scale of their numbers in what must be the largest single academic market in the world. The sociology of peace processes, however, has no popular following. I have always wanted to engage sociologists, showing what our discipline illuminates about the topic of peace. Peace, however, is not immediately thought of as sociological, not part of our conceptual armoury; not taught in our curricula, and not featuring in the pages of our journals. My engagement with sociologists on the topic of peace has thus been mostly through books (Brewer 2003, 2010; Brewer, Higgins and Teeney 2011; Brewer, Mitchell and Leavey 2013; Brewer, Hayes and Teeney 2018; Brewer et al. 2018; Brewer and Wahidin 2021). This volume is another.

It is deeply paradoxical, however, to write another book to resist disciplinary closure when most sociologists no longer work in a book culture. This is a measure of my difficulty in writing this text and of the ambitions I have for it. Part of this difficulty is the nature of 'advanced introductions' themselves. Advanced introductions to subject areas come in at least two types. Mostly they are magisterial overviews of large fields in which the author offers a fresh perspective on a crowded literature, and which takes account of latest developments. Occasionally, however, they are primers for a new field of intellectual endeavour, laying down a programmatic overview of a fresh subject area. The objective of this *Advanced Introduction to the Sociology of Peace Processes* is clearly the latter. It is not an overview of the literature on peace processes in political science, peace studies, human rights law, theology, transitional justice studies or international relations studies, to name a few of the disciplines that lay claim to expertise on the subject. The aim is to advance the claims of a sociological approach to peace processes, introducing what sociology has to add to the inter-disciplinary focus on peace processes. This is not academic imperialism. Sociology cannot tell us all we need to know about the process of conflict transformation; this *Advanced Introduction* shows what a sociological imagination contributes new to the analysis of peace processes.

Individual sociologists have played a significant role in peace studies, conflict resolution and related fields. For example, the founder of peace studies as a discipline, Johan Galtung, is a mathematical sociologist. Sociology has a strong presence in Bradford University's Department of Peace Studies and International Development, including in the work of Paul Rogers and Tom Woodhouse. One of the world's most celebrated conflict resolution

INTRODUCTION: AN AUTOBIOGRAPHY OF THE BOOK 3

experts, John Paul Lederach, is a sociologist. Sociologists contribute significantly to our understanding of non-violent action (Kurtz and Smithey 2018), the political sociology of peace (Goetze and de Guevara 2021), transitional justice (Elster 2004), trauma (Alexander 2012), and religious peacebuilding (Beck 2010). The sociologist Anthony Oberschall (2007) has pioneered the analysis of conflict and peace in divided societies where they wrestle with ethnic divisions. Sociologists have documented the link between violence, peace and vulnerability (Misztal 2011a; Turner 2006; Wilkinson and Kleinman 2016), violence, love and hate (Scheff 2011b), and the added features of the sociology of suffering (Wilkinson 2005). Some sociologists have been key activists in conflict zones as practitioners, notably Baruch Kimmerling in Israel–Palestine (Kimmerling 2012), and Fatima Meer (2017) and Eddie Webster in South Africa (on Webster, see Burawoy 2010). However, none codified their practice into a programmatic outline of a sociology of peace processes. The practice of sociology in peace studies has not generated a sociology of the practice of peace. What follows is one such attempt.

It is necessary to add a cautionary note. I have written extensively on the topics covered here in numerous publications over a long career, some of which are hard to access or are now out of print. I reference this work copiously for those readers who care to follow up the elaborations. I apologise in advance for referring excessively to this work, but this short book cannot provide the details I have given elsewhere; it is hard to write short books when there is so much to say in a programmatic argument. This volume has the advantage, however, of crystallising my arguments, bringing them together in one place, and employing a writing style that makes them accessible to lay readers. They have also not been read by sociologists from outside the field, with whom I wish to engage through this volume.

2 From the sociologies of order and conflict to the sociologies of war and peace

Introduction

This chapter charts the history of sociology's engagement with issues of order, conflict and peace. It shows the transition from early sociological concerns with order, to the emergence of a sociology of conflict, and a sociology of war and violence. The sociology of war and violence alerts us to the sociological features of new forms of war in the global era. The chapter argues that the deeply moral nature of new forms of war opens up an intellectual space for discussing the political economy of the moral reawakening of interest in peace. The emergence of 'new wars', and the moral reaction to them, is the discipline's opportunity to develop a sociology of peace processes.

The sociology of order

The origins of sociology are highly contested, but it is indisputable that the discipline took huge strides forward in times of rapid social upheaval and change, when sociologists operating without the name, offered an analysis of the human and social condition. Antecedents can be traced as far back as we find people thinking and writing about moral sentiments and group life. A self-conscious sociology, however, needs a sense of the social, separate from the sacred and the state, in which society is the

FROM THE SOCIOLOGIES OF ORDER AND CONFLICT 5

product of action rather than design, whether divine or contract. This isolation of the social did not fully arise until the Enlightenment in the eighteenth century (thus Ray's 1999: 192 theorisation of the classical tradition in sociology, for example, argues that sociology was a debate with the Enlightenment). The Scottish variant of the Enlightenment marks the beginnings of modern reflections in Britain that can rightly be considered as sociological (Brewer 2014a).

The spur to this sociological effervescence in Scotland was the rapid social change the Lowlands were undergoing in the eighteenth century. There was urban relocation from the Highlands; new town planning in Edinburgh and Glasgow; the growth of commercialism and proto-industrialism ahead of England, changing the nature of work and of social relations based on work; the emergence of sharp divisions in social class, referred to then as social rank, linked to the social division of labour; growing inequalities around gender, class, occupation and wealth; and the emergence of what later generations came to call exploitation (Brewer 1986a) and alienation.

Adam Ferguson's work in particular is concentrated on the negative consequences of these social changes for people's human nature, their identification with each other, and their state of happiness, what today we would call their sociability and what he called the social band. Ferguson was very good at analysing the threats to sociability arising from the new social conditions embedded in proto-industrialism, but he was very weak in advocating ways in which sociability might be recreated, mentioning only sport and new forms of association, like militias. The threats to good order were analysed with great sociological insight. What Ferguson lacked was the sociological vision for how order might be recreated. It was, if you like, a sociology of critique, not advocacy of social order by means of sociology.

The sociologists of the nineteenth century, by which time the name had been invented in France by Comte, extended the critique of what was by then full-blown industrialisation and were much more sociologically attuned to its forms of amelioration. Sociology became in the work of many in the nineteenth century a form of conservative advocacy of social order, with society itself the solution to disorder. This gave us what Robert Nisbet (1967) termed the unit ideas of sociology – the sacred, community,

6   ADVANCED INTRODUCTION TO THE SOCIOLOGY OF PEACE PROCESSES

authority, status, and alienation – that shaped the discipline's concern with order and stability amidst rapid social change.

There was still critique of the negative effects of industrialisation, but primarily not focused on the Scots' concern with weakened sociability and human unhappiness, but for threats to social cohesion. The late Geoffrey Hawthorne's depiction of the history of sociology is thus entitled *Enlightenment and Despair* (2008), capturing the sense of opportunity and threat posed by industrialism. Nisbet therefore conceived of his unit ideas each having an anti-thesis, the contrast between them representing aspects of order and disorder. Senses of community were thus threatened by anomic society, legitimate authority by power, traditional status by new social class, the sacred by secularisation, and with senses of alienation embedded in the obsession with blind progress. *The Sociological Tradition* was a diagnosis of the threat to social cohesion and social order by the release of society from tradition. It was essentially conservative, emphasising the positive effects in society of values like community, the established status hierarchy, religion and authority. The sociology of order was thus facilitated by modernisation as a form of advocacy for social cohesion.

By addressing itself to the central question of how social order is created and maintained when cohesion is under threat from social change, the focus was on the key social institutions, social structures, social behaviours and social values that aligned to ensure society maintained the status quo or evolved slowly rather than changed radically. Some advocates of the sociology of order were attracted to the discipline precisely because they were against modernism and industrialisation and saw in sociology an intellectual framework for their conservative philosophies and religious views (Nisbet 1973). Sociology in Britain at the turn of the nineteenth century, for example, had adherents from High Anglicans and Catholics, who felt it gave justification to their resistance against progress, seeing in the sociological writings of Le Play, as one instance, a holy trinity of pre-industrial pastoralism, Catholicism, and agrarian community (Brewer 2007).

As sociology professionalised as a discipline in the twentieth century, the sociological framework through which social order was understood, was expanded into what Dawe (1970: 208) referred to as the doctrine of the sociology of the social system. This was more than a set of theoretical ideas; it is a whole universe of values, beliefs and meanings for sociological concepts and theories that shaped meta-theoretical and empirical levels of analysis. The sociology of the social system, for example, bequeathed the discipline with theoretical ideas that dominated sociology up to the 1960s, like functionalism, as well as substantive analyses of the mechanisms of social order, like roles, socialisation, culture, community and authority. Sociologists of the social system, such as Parsons and Shills, dominated the discipline, conceiving of society as an internally regulated system to maintain social cohesion, with an image of people as 'homo sociologicus' (Abell 1991; Archer 2000a; Boudon 2006), over-socialised and obedient (Wrong 1961).

It is no coincidence that this met its zenith in US sociology in the 1950s, a society so fragmented, ethnically diverse and culturally differentiated that the sociology of order was mobilised as an advocacy for how order is maintained out of potential chaos in societies like the USA. This kind of sociology dominated the discipline world-wide, only because the later introduction of sociology elsewhere led to the initial globalisation of US sociology in the curriculum, and in practice and research. Sociology, however, was about to change as society itself underwent radical transformation.

The sociology of conflict

The paradox for the sociology of order is that embedded in sociology's conservative anti-modernism, are other forms of critique. Sociological analysis of the negative effects of industrialisation equally sustains radical critiques that advocate the positive effects of social change; it is not too much change that blights the social condition, but not enough change. This was the language of nineteenth-century conflict sociologists like Gumplowicz (on which, see Brewer 2014a).

The sociology of conflict is a form of advocacy that mobilises sociological ideas for the purpose of social change. It is social change, not social cohesion, that ameliorates the negative effects of modernisation and industrialisation. It is not, of course, a form of advocacy of violence; the two sides of its Janus face address, on the one hand, the oppressiveness and stultifying character of excessive forms of cohesion, and on the other,

8   ADVANCED INTRODUCTION TO THE SOCIOLOGY OF PEACE PROCESSES

the positive social effects of some forms of conflict (see Coser 1956 on the functions of conflict). These two dimensions are linked. Excessive cohesion can provoke conflict because it is experienced as oppressiveness, even repression, and conflict can have instrumental value in society by promoting social change and reform. The sociology of war, for example, has as a central tenet the idea that war drives social progress and social reform (Malesevic 2010).

As Anthony Smith (1976: 7) once put it, while there is a logical priority of persistence over change, substantively, entities change so much that change has a striking predominance (1976: 8), especially since the industrial era. To others, however, struggle, not cohesion, is the defining motif of society, and it takes logical priority. Within the sociology of conflict, it is struggle against inequality, injustice, unfairness, oppression, authoritarianism and the like that solves the problems of modernisation and industrialisation by radical transformation of social institutions, structures, behaviours and values. This involves an analysis of how society is organised to promote and protect the material, cultural and symbolic power of a minority against the majority, as well as an analysis of how social change can be motivated to achieve radical reform of society, to promote and protect the interests of the oppressed through the means by which people seek to take back control.

The groupings in conflict were first conceived in class terms, especially amongst adherents of Marx, but now they also cohere around social cleavages of ethnicity, 'race', religion, nationality, gender, sexuality, culture and the like. In this manner, for example, contemporary conflict sociology merges with critical feminist analysis, to explain both the forces that maintain gender inequality and the processes for how this can be changed. This is true also for critical race analysis, post-colonial studies and 'queer sociology', to name a few. The example of 'queer sociology' is indicative of contemporary conflict analysis. While the word 'queer' is often a derogatory reference to LGBT identity, 'queer sociology' analyses how power intersects with race, class, gender, colonialism and sexuality to structure identities and their inequalities. It is as applicable to racial hierarchies as ones of sexuality (Moussawi and Vidal-Ortiz 2020).

In the sociology of conflict, competition, struggle and resistance are used to explain macro social phenomena, such as war, poverty, colonialism, climate inequalities and revolution, as well as everyday life micro-conflicts, like violence in the home, gender violence, and harassment and discrimination. Rex (1981), for example, begins his exploration of social conflict with an analysis of the micro-sociology of conflict. However, conflict, competition, struggle and resistance are also social processes that are said to drive the movement of history and progress in society. This is why Rex moves from micro-conflicts to conflicts in social systems. Studies of the social consequences of particular and notable instances of social conflict – forms of collective violence, riot, war, civil unrest, revolution throughout history – abound in the sociology of conflict because they demonstrate that competition, not cohesion, is the hallmark of society and the motivation for social change. As an exile from apartheid South Africa, Rex may well have had his homeland in mind when developing a paradigm for conflict analysis in sociology (1981: 123–5), nomenclature which deliberately evoked earlier reflections in the USA on the functionalist and social system paradigms in sociology. Similarly, Coser used the functionalist language of Parsons to advocate the sociology of conflict (Coser 1956; see also Jaworski 1991).

Transcending the two sociologies debate

The reconstruction of the discipline of sociology as a tension between the two sociologies of order and conflict, owes much to Alan Dawe's (1970) influential argument that its history reflects a simple binary divide between the focus on consensus and order, or control and conflict. The spaces of its production and reading are significant to Dawe's analysis. It was published on the back of the massive growth in sociology in the UK, with the expansion of university education after the 1963 Robbins Report, where sociology proved popular in the new universities, as well as the introduction in schools and further education colleges of sociology as an 'A' and 'O' Level subject. Sociology lacked a grounding in the traditional universities and in the school curriculum, so the large number of new adherents needed to discover sociology's history rather hurriedly. The two sociologies debate provided them with that socialisation, accounting for the whole of the discipline's antecedents and its major formative figures. Dawe's argument proved popular for its simplicity, accessibility and comprehensiveness.

10   ADVANCED INTRODUCTION TO THE SOCIOLOGY OF PEACE PROCESSES

There are two main problems with Dawe's argument. The first is relatively uncontentious: there are more than two sociologies, and these other sociologies do not squeeze satisfactorily into the binary. The second complaint is that the contrast between order and conflict is not a binary at all, for consensus and change are parts of the same social process.

The so-called cognitivist revolution that occurred in sociology in the 1960s was based, not on the problems of social order or social control, but on the problem of social meaning. It motivated a rejection of conventional sociological theorising and empirical practice in its search for how people constructed their own realities, through the social meanings they attribute to the social world and the people and situations they encounter. Cognitivist sociology took several forms, many of which had long antecedents, such as symbolic interactionism, rooted in 1920s Chicago School sociology, social phenomenology, based on Schutz's writings from the 1930s–1950s, ethnomethodology, and a variety of different sociologies of everyday life (Douglas et al. 1980). Everyday life is the realm in which ordinary, taken-for-granted, habitual social life is performed, experienced and understood as ordinary, taken-for-granted and habitual (Brewer et al. 2018: 15–17), so the focus is on ways of thinking about society's structures, institutions and values, and their meanings, rather than reifying these structures as objective realities. It was this cognitivist type of sociology, as much as Dawe's characterisation, that provoked Ted Benton's (1978) critique of the two sociologies debate by charting what he called the third sociology, based around critical realism, a view that argues for an objective reality independent of people's social meanings. As sociology has developed into the new millennium, there is now a multiplicity of sociologies to challenge the depiction of the discipline as divided merely into two binary universes of meaning and value.

The more serious challenge to Dawe's argument is that order and conflict are not mutually exclusive, but recursively linked as two sides of the one social process. Cohesion and order are indivisible from competition and conflict. Inasmuch as sociology portrays the relationship between structure and agency – which is the modern rendering of the debate over two sociologies – as recursive (Giddens 1984), this is how we must also see the relationship between order and conflict.

To understand this, we must illustrate the recursiveness between structure and agency. Structure defines the recurring social institutions which influence the opportunities available to people, determining pathways to action and choice in social life as a constraint on free will. Agency is the capacity of individuals to act independently and to make their own free choices, separate from the structures and institutions within which their social lives are conducted. Many modern sociologists have engaged in the debate over structure and agency (Walsh 1998); it parallels the earlier discourse over order and conflict as a way of characterising the universe of meaning in sociological theorising and empirical practice. The point, however, is that structure and agency are not mutually exclusive but implicate each other. As Giddens (1984) famously argued, an understanding of both agency and structure is necessary regardless of the empirical or theoretical issue at hand, since they are part of a single process of interaction, linked recursively and presupposing each other. Structures are simultaneously constraints on people's agency by imposing limits on their capacity for action, but also an enablement by empowering people into forms of action that transcend and transform these constraints. Agency thus constitutes the structure that both constrains and enables further agency. This was described by Giddens as the 'duality of structure', in which structure is constituted by, yet constrains, agency (for an example of how this is operationalised to understand membership of the British Union of Fascists, see Brewer 1988).

In similar fashion, order and conflict implicate each other and are part of a single interactive process. Sociologists have long successfully demonstrated their recursive relationship. Two examples can suffice. Adam Ferguson, for example, emphasised how sport mediated what he referred to as people's 'militaristic spirit', constituting a form of democratic translation of competition, conflict and control, so as to facilitate sociability and cohesion. It is from this analysis that Ferguson's work was taken up by conflict sociologists, such as Gumplowicz, first in Germany and then the USA (Brewer 2014a: 12). However, Durkheim's sociology is perhaps the premier example. Universally recognised as one of the founders of the classical tradition of sociology (unlike Ferguson), his depiction of the threat of anomie – normlessness – in modern societies, led him to the argument that conflict with an out-group can enhance cohesion of the in-group, realising new forms of normative behaviour and identification (Marks 1974). Durkheim believed that diminished solidarity was a pathological condition and that modern societies needed to reinforce social norms. Paradoxically, one way of doing this is found in conflict and war. The more cohesive the group, the more it provokes hostility with equally

12   ADVANCED INTRODUCTION TO THE SOCIOLOGY OF PEACE PROCESSES

cohesive out-groups, confronting each other as two solidaristic groups in competition over nation, territory, resources or support. In short, conflict can be instrumental in enhancing cohesiveness, and cohesiveness can provoke conflict.

This is an observation with general application. Repression of social groups and social movements by powerful others can augment their social cohesiveness and eliminate internal fissures. This simultaneously facilitates internal co-operation which can invigorate conflict with these powerful others. Such links motivated a great deal of the interest in crowd behaviour in sociology and psychology in the wake of Nazism; ironically, it is the cohesiveness of crowd psychology that mobilises the crowd to concerted acts of resistance, violence and unrest. The Rwandan genocide, for example, has been analysed in terms of collective fear within one group, which mobilised them as a cohesive group to engage in genocidal acts of conflict against another (McDoom 2012). In a similar way, the internal cohesiveness of a negotiating party seeking to resolve conflict, can improve the negotiating process and encourage a peaceful outcome. It is often argued, for example, that negotiations leading to the Good Friday Agreement in Northern Ireland were facilitated by the internal cohesiveness of Loyalist paramilitary groups under the Combined Loyalist Command, ensuring a single voice and a single body with which to negotiate, a unity that has subsequently dissolved (on the sociology of the Northern Irish peace process, see Brewer 2018a).

Empirically, therefore, order and conflict are indissoluble, recursively linked as part of one social process. We can call this social process 'sociability', the process by which people with self-interests and personal preferences learn to live together and relate meaningfully with each other. People are, as Runciman (1999) reminded us, 'social animals' and are communal beings (Studdart 2016). The moral order of society, as Frisby and Sayer (1986: 42) once described it, means much more than that groups have moral sentiments; it is that societies must continually reproduce sociability. This is not just about moral cohesion and the typical concerns of the sociology of order; it presupposes order and competition, cohesiveness and conflict.

Moral cohesion cannot exist without distributive fairness, social justice, equality of opportunity and compromise. Johan Galtung (1969) referred to injustice, poverty, discrimination, unfairness and the like as a form of structural violence, which fed his view that 'positive peace' required social transformation to realise justice, equality of opportunity and distributive fairness. Ignatieff (2017) refers to these as 'ordinary virtues' (and Elias 2000 [1939], the 'civilising process'). Significantly, their absence can provoke conflict, in much the same manner that Fiske and Rai (2015) describe some forms of violence as virtuous, as many ex-combatants are wont to do (with respect to Northern Irish ex-combatants, see Brewer 2021a, 2021c). Yet, as Ignatieff wished to demonstrate, the recreation of these ordinary virtues after conflict is a way of restoring sociability and the moral order of society. This is the thrust of my argument elsewhere that most first-generation victims of conflict are moral beacons, as a result of the magnanimity they show towards erstwhile enemies (Brewer 2018b: 236–41; Brewer and Hayes 2011b; Brewer, Hayes and Teeney 2018).

In short, the moral order of society requires the reproduction of sociability, which in itself presupposes both order and conflict as indivisible components of moral sensibility. The same indissolubility is true for war and peace. Whilst sociologists have been productive in outlining the well-defined field of the sociology of war and violence, its indissoluble partner in the couplet, the sociology of peace, has been neglected. In the next section, therefore, we begin documenting sociology's interest in violence and war.

The sociology of violence and war

Sociology's interest in violence shows itself in concern with particular spaces of violence. These are physical, symbolic and cultural spaces where violence is routine, such as in the domestic sphere, or where it is common or newly emerging, such as religious terrorism, ethnic violence, gender and sexual violence, everyday life micro-violence, wars of decolonisation and racial violence. Sociology has isolated different types of violence, such as interpersonal violence, crowd behaviour and collective violence, revolution, civil unrest, micro-violence, genocide, criminal violence, structural violence and the like. These are interdisciplinary fields, but the contribution of sociologists has been influential, for example in the analysis of patriarchy and male violence (Walby 1989, 1990) and genocide (Chalk and Jonassohn 1990; Shaw 2007). There are also sociological the-

14   ADVANCED INTRODUCTION TO THE SOCIOLOGY OF PEACE PROCESSES

orisations of violence (see, for example, Ray 2018; Walby 2013, 2021) and of war (for example, Kaldor 1999; Malesevic 2010; Münkler 2005).

This work shows that violence has not declined with modernity, as first argued; it is ubiquitous, embedded in the social fabric (Ray 2018: 3). Modernity is consistent with various forms of mass violence, from the Holocaust (Bauman 1991) to Cambodia and Rwanda, which moved sociologists to reflect, for example, on the role of religion in managing the aftermath of mass atrocities (Brudholm and Cushman 2009). While the nation state once had a monopoly of the means of violence, the proliferation of armed groups, and their easy access to armed technologies, has seen violence dispersed throughout global society. Nation states, however, can themselves be particularly violent in abusing human rights, breaching the rule of law they are supposed to defend to create a crisis of legitimacy, particularly in the context of decolonisation and in new anti-democratic regimes in the Global South. This is why we need new conceptualisations of legitimacy that morally sustain participation in 'virtuous violence' (Brewer 2021a: 98–103).

Neo-liberal governance has also provoked renewed violence (Walby 2021), such as in the Global North, as competition for resources escalates with the narrowing of the welfare state, and as the new forms of authoritarian populism it has encouraged inflame old cleavages and promote new identity concerns. Violence is not restricted to the margins of society therefore, nor to peripheral social groups. Sociology has also made us aware that some forms of violence continued through the process of modernisation, never to decline, such as domestic violence, and gendered and sexual violence. Ethnic violence, genocidal violence and religious violence, for example, also show continuity over time in the wake of the growth of independence movements following the Second World War, the collapse of communism, and decolonisation in the Global South.

This has moved the study of violence to the core of the discipline. This is reflected in two shifts that distinguish warfare in late modernity. The first is the rise of new forms of organised violence, that have simultaneously destroyed the distinction between 'combatant' and 'civilian' and increased the level of barbarity and atrocity experienced by innocent people, especially women (Hayner 2010). Moses (2021) traces the collapse of this distinction to the West rather than to the rise of despotic, geocidal regimes in the Global South, especially US-led regional wars against

FROM THE SOCIOLOGIES OF ORDER AND CONFLICT 15

communism that targeted whole populations. With no set battle site now, the human body has become a battleground, subjected to cruel forms of moral degradation (Hynes 2004).

The second shift is the growth of international regulatory structures and global civil society that both monitor the conduct of war and proffer modes of intervention to impose peace processes (Atack 2005; Hirsch 2003). It is in this context that the sociology of war concerns itself with new forms of warfare. Mary Kaldor's (1999) argument to this effect has spurred scholarship that identifies that some 'new' practices of war have been ever present (see, particularly, Moses 2021; Münkler 2005), but it is incontrovertible that some forms of war have changed dramatically and are on the increase (Shaw 2005), and Kaldor (2013) has strongly defended her argument.

The sociological significance of new wars is that they, in effect, create moral injuries. In the existing literature in psychology (Nichter et al. 2021) moral injuries are injuries to a victim's moral codes, causing added emotional and psychological damage.[1] Moral injuries in a sociological sense are injuries inflicted because of moral codes, where combatants engage in particularly barbarous atrocities because the enemy is morally enervated and stripped of moral worth and dignity.

This is the context in which we can locate the sociology of peace processes. While war and peace implicate each other, for no war is irresolvable and no peace secure from renewed conflict (Brewer 2010: 8), the sociology of peace processes is more securely embedded in the discipline than as a mere reverse image of war. It must be located in what, elsewhere, I have called the re-enchantment of the social sciences following their second cognitivist revolution (Brewer and Hayes 2011a: 8–9). The first cognitivist revolution was the rediscovery of social meaning in the intellectual shift against the sociology of the social system and its positivist methodology in the 1960s; the second is the re-emergence of interest in moral sensibility.

The re-enchantment of the social sciences

The social sciences underwent a process of *dis*enchantment as part of their professionalisation in the late nineteenth and twentieth centuries.

16   ADVANCED INTRODUCTION TO THE SOCIOLOGY OF PEACE PROCESSES

The social sciences emerged out of moral philosophy in the eighteenth century, and early social science discourses were replete with moral concerns. As we have already argued, the great advance in sociology in the Scottish Enlightenment in the eighteenth century, for example, was motivated by an intellectual concern to demonstrate the distorting effect of social conditions on the inherent sociability of human nature. Nor was it unusual, for instance, to find examples of Christian sociology on the bookshelves and curricula of British and US universities in the late nineteenth century (for a modern example of Christian sociology, see Scimecca 2019). Britain's first sociological society at the beginning of the twentieth century had clergy as members, and the early *Sociological Review* published their work right up to the 1920s. Indeed, a little-known journal of Christian sociology called *Christendom* ran in Britain from 1930 to 1959 (see Brewer 2007 for elaboration). Cultural relics like *Christendom* can last only so long however, and as the social sciences separated into disciplinary silos by the mid-twentieth century and became professional, especially with the growth of new universities in the 1960s, they reproduced what here I call disenchantment.

I take my definition of disenchantment from the German sociologist Max Weber, meaning the emphasis on rationality and rationalisation (see Bendix 1966, who makes rationalisation the key to his intellectual portrait of Weber; see also Weber (1968 [1921]). Rationalisation denudes culture, society and politics of an interest in the emotional and cognitive. Disenchantment within twentieth-century social science was manifested in three particular ways: a methodological emphasis on objectivity that separated the personal from professional practice, and forbad any ethical commitments; a theoretical concern with cultural relativism that encouraged a moral disregard for evil, harm, suffering and injustice as morally absolute categories; and a value orientation that favoured technocratic and scientific mentality over moral sensibility. Incidentally, this led to highly secularised discourse and ethically impoverished debates (with respect to what I disparagingly call the 'sociology of secularisation', see Brewer 2019).

This disavowal of moral sensibility is no better expressed than by C. Wright Mills, the doyen of radical critics of social science in the 1950s, when he described the human condition in the following way: 'Facts now outrun sensibility. In official man there is no more human shock; in the unofficial follower there is little sense of moral issue. Within the

FROM THE SOCIOLOGIES OF ORDER AND CONFLICT 17

unopposed supremacy of impersonal, calculated technique, there is no human place to draw the line and give the emphatic no' (Mills 1959a: 83; for Mills' writings on war and peace, see Brewer 2013b, 2021d). While Mills was primarily complaining about the lack of moral sensibility in the mid-twentieth-century USA, this was a general criticism. Three-quarters of a century later and the human condition is quite different. Vulnerability, risk and threats to human dignity abound, forcing sociology and the social sciences to develop new conceptual interests.

A few random examples of this kind of work will have to suffice. The sociologist Barbara Misztal (2011a), for example, has written extensively on the sociology of vulnerability, along with Bryan Turner (2006). The philosopher and theologian Nicholas Wolterstorff (2008) made human dignity central to his theory of human rights, and the ethicist Avishai Margalit (2010) made it central to his identification of what he called rotten political compromise agreements. The sociology of shame has moved from considerations of personal stigma of the self towards group analysis, violent conflict and fractures to the social bond (Scheff 2000, 2011a). Hope has reappeared in the sociological lexicon (for example, Davies 2010; Petersen and Wilkinson 2015; Plummer 2015), as well as love and hate (Scheff 2011b), and the British Sociological Association has a study group focused on the sociology of happiness. Martha Nussbaum's discussion in *Political Emotions* (2013), for example, has the subtitle *Why Love Matters for Justice*, in which she makes compassion for the suffering of others, what she calls love, the basic human emotion. There is renewed interest in the ethical foundations to the public value of the social sciences (Brewer 2013a), and of what Flanagan (1996) calls sociology's 'enchantment' through its re-engagement with theology. One of Britain's best-known social theorists, Margaret Archer (2000b), wrote a treatise on what it means to be human. And there has been a Christianisation of social science discourse as some practitioners consciously locate their work in Christian values and ideas, including debates about Christian love, forgiveness, and healing after conflict. There is now an array of cognitivist concerns in modern social science that reflect a reawakening of interest in moral sensibility, in themes like resentment, suffering, reconciliation, anger, love, shame, suffering, hope, empathy, revenge, compassion, forgiveness, healing, compromise and the like. The sociology of emotions gives full expression to this kind of work in all aspects of social behaviour and social relations (see, for example, Stets and Turner 2006),

18   ADVANCED INTRODUCTION TO THE SOCIOLOGY OF PEACE PROCESSES

not just with respect to conflict (but on this, see Brewer 2010: 103–40; Elster 2004; Scheff 1994, 2011a, 2011b; Scheff and Ratzinger 1991).

As a sociologist, I locate the re-enchantment of the social sciences in structural and material conditions that have reawakened interest in moral sensibility and accordingly refreshed the conceptual field of sociology. There is, if you like, a political economy to moral sensibility into which this re-enchantment fits. Late modernity is characterised by great technological advances, but also by significantly increased vulnerabilities and inequalities. I want to emphasise five features of what I call the political economy of re-enchantment.

1. Late modernity is characterised by an extremely violent hegemonic globalisation which, paradoxically, accords itself a moral role in resolving local and regional conflicts by universalising liberal notions of peace and Western democracy. Smith (2021) refers to this as the globalisation of peace. Global capitalism creates competitive territorial states which institutionalise expropriation, exploitation and extraction, incentivising national self-interest and greed, into which the growth of inter-state violence must be located. This also explains the rise in organised violence by non-state actors who resist hegemonic globalisation. At the same time, localised subaltern groups grant themselves moral virtue by resisting hegemonic globalisation in their specific context but, paradoxically, often use violence to challenge cultural and economic globalisation despite their discourse of peace and social justice. Hegemonic globalisation, in other words, implicates a language of peace, if not its practice. This was emphasised by Beck (2010) in his sojourn into the sociology of religion, when he characterised the reflexive nature of modernity as facilitating the growth of individualised, non-institutional religious forms ('gods of our own making') which replace divine transcendence with a focus on peace.

2. Late modernity's hegemonic globalisation has increased wealth disparities and depletion of the Global South, but also impoverishes growing sections of the Global North, left behind as casualties of neo-liberal capitalist economics. The concentration of wealth in fewer and fewer hands is matched by increasing vulnerabilities amongst the rest, and increased risks to global economic trends, to climate change, and to organised violence, amongst others. Late modernity is a risk society, as sociologists argue (Beck 2010; Wilkinson and Kleinman 2016), with increased risks and increased sensitivities to risk. With

increased risk comes a sense of increased vulnerability. Late modernity has become aware of what Bauman (1998) calls the *in*human consequences of globalisation. The lived experience of globalisation is not just one of new opportunities of hope; it is simultaneously one of fear, anxiety, suffering, hate and genocidal othering.

3. As we have argued earlier, the growth in organised violence and its changing nature in late modernity have led both to more war and to an increase in morally degrading forms of violence in 'new wars' (Kaldor 1999, 2013). New wars are not between identifiable armies on set battlefields observing the Geneva Conventions of war. There is no longer a distinction between civilian and combatant, and the human body has been turned into a battlefield. Moral enervation of the enemy – stripping them of human dignity – has led both to the wide availability of sophisticated weaponry to attack whole communities, as well as the use of de-technological forms of weaponry against the human body, with de-humanising moral degradations inflicted on it. This has seen the return of the machete and sword as weapons of war. The use of the body as a weapon in mass suicide bombings is another reflection of this de-humanised, moral degradation. The return of moral sensibility in social science in late modernity is, in part, the return of genocidal violence to contemporary experience.

4. There has been a collapse in the public–private distinction in late modernity, in which public space has been domesticated, with a range of behaviours and emotions once reserved for the private sphere now entering public and political discourse (for how this collapse links to the sociology of compromise, see Brewer 2018c: 13–16). The language of modern politics in the public sphere is the language of emotion, religion, identity, authenticity and, in some cases, hate. Hate speech, xenophobia, and ethnic and religious othering has been normalised by a public discourse by politicians and media broadcasters that has rendered victims' suffering into entertainment or political rhetoric. The penetration of formerly private emotions into the public sphere has turned shame, outrage and offence into public display.

5. This fear of 'the enemy within' is matched by a feeling of moral responsibility to strangers and to what Boltanski (1999) calls their 'distant suffering' (see also Wilkinson 2005); but only so long as they remain distant. Globalisation compresses time and space in a way that brings the distant suffering of others into people's living rooms and their social media screens and smart phones, to the point where images of distant suffering bombard late modernity and underpin

significant and increased philanthropic and charitable giving. When the stranger ends up on our shores as refugees and migrants, however, or gets to sleep in doorways on our rich streets, the collapse of the distance turns the stranger into the enemy within, and any moral sensibility is restrained. It is for this reason that late modernity is morally contradictory, as moral responsibility to the 'distant other' is matched by anti-foreigner sentiment and aggressive xenophobia. This is why Sylvia Wynter (1999), the Caribbean novelist and anti-colonial social thinker, refers to what she calls 'the re-enchantment of humanism' to describe the moral framework in which there are no racial and colonial categorisations.

The political economy of re-enchantment has, at one and the same time, increased moral sensibility to suffering, harm and the human consequences of the social condition *and* increased the moral enervation and moral degradation of our enemies. We are both sensitive to the suffering of strangers and fearful of them. We show greater levels of emotional empathy to people just like ourselves but draw ever more rigid boundaries to exclude those who are different, even to the extent of using barbarous violence against them. Moral sensibility and moral enervation are parallel social processes in late modernity. Migrant children therefore get washed up dead on our holiday beaches drowned with people's sorrow, but otherwise with no practical effect.

Two things follow for sociology. First, the conceptual apparatus of sociology has changed to make sense of the changed conditions of late modernity, so the currency of our discourse is now one that debates themes like social suffering, human dignity, anger, hope, empathy, forgiveness, love, hate and all the rest. We have seen the return of moral sensibility, precisely because the commitment of previous generations to the idea of progress has been challenged by the very process of rationalisation itself that makes these concepts relevant again. In short, re-enchantment has renewed the conceptual field of our discipline.

Second, sociology has lost the sense of itself as providing immaculate perception, the single virgin analysis. Sociology shares the intellectual discussion of moral sensibility with other disciplines, including theology and other social sciences, but also climate scientists, philosophers, oceanographers, psychoanalysts, humanities scholars and the like. The re-enchantment of the social sciences therefore promotes inter-disciplinarity rather than disciplinary silos (on the rise of sociological insight in religious studies, see, for example, Brewer 2007; in international relations, see Goetze and de Guevara 2021; Wallis 2021). In short, re-enchantment means we need to rethink the boundaries of sociology. This has implications for the sociology of peace processes.

Conclusion

Peace is sociological. Peace and war are universal processes in society and presuppose each other in the same way as do order and conflict; they are part of the same concern with moral sensibility. Moral sensibility describes the process by which people live together in sociability despite ubiquitous competition, conflict and violence. The moral reawakening of sociology and the social sciences in late modernity, linked to a political economy that promotes an interest in moral sensibility, has opened up an intellectual space for a whole new conceptual vocabulary in sociology and social science generally that reflects what I call its re-enchantment. Peace is part of that sociological landscape.

However, an interest in peace has largely been absent in sociology's renewed engagement with moral sensibility, with its focus more on violence and its many manifestations. In 2013, I laid down a complaint that there was not much work on peace processes going on in sociology (Brewer 2013c: 163), or at least, it was hived off into new inter-disciplinary sub-fields like memory studies, victimology, transitional justice studies and the like. In these ways, sociology is an exporter discipline, sending its practitioners to infuse inter-disciplinary fields. I made the point that part of the problem in establishing the sociology of peace processes is not so much hostility from outsiders, but persuading sociologists that our discipline has something to contribute in the face of its disciplinary fragmentation, to which the new field of the sociology of peace processes might be thought itself to contribute.

A sociology of peace processes, however, must be one that shares its interests, concerns and concepts with cognate disciplines. In this respect, sociology illuminates a great deal about peace that has hitherto remained secondary or hidden in the disciplines that dominate its analysis, while inter-disciplinary engagements with the topic offer sociology new collaborative opportunities across disciplinary boundaries, from which the discipline can learn a great deal. In the next chapter, therefore, we begin to reflect on what is sociological about peace, in order to begin this inter-disciplinary conversation.

NOTE

1.   I owe this insight to Kisane Prutton from the University of Derby.

3 Understanding what peace means sociologically

Introduction

This chapter outlines sociology's clarification of the meaning of peace and peace processes. It delineates the concepts involved in peace – active versus passive peace, negative versus positive peace, conflict transformation versus social transformation, statebuilding versus peacebuilding, and the political peace process versus the social peace process. The chapter then identifies what is sociological about peace processes and their various types, offering a typology based on three sociological axes. It focuses on the special problems surrounding one type of peace process, the mutually agreed second preference deal that is called the compromise type. The chapter ends by isolating what new concepts and ideas sociology furnishes to the field.

What is peace?

Peace is widely thought to mean the outbreak of agreement. This is not so. Political disagreements mostly remain as trenchant as before; what peace means is that these disagreements are now pursued by non-violent means. Nor is peace necessarily unanimously popular. As I have written in the past, peace comes with costs (Brewer 2010: 30–36). However, peace has such universal appeal that it is rarely disavowed in public. Who, after all, is prepared to admit they dislike mothers and apple pies? What elsewhere I have called the problem of expectations (Brewer 2015b), means that erstwhile enemies rarely say publicly that they oppose change; they

24   ADVANCED INTRODUCTION TO THE SOCIOLOGY OF PEACE PROCESSES

expect the other, however, to do all the changing. They themselves have nothing to change; 'not an inch' as some Northern Irish Unionists say.

At a minimum level, peace means the absence of violence, conflict and war. However, this does not say very much about the level of public commitment to the peacefulness that defines the absence of war, nor much about people's obligation to make the changes necessary to continue abstaining from war. Peace properly understood is not the *absence* of something, but the *presence* of something. To begin to clarify some of the ambiguities surrounding the concept, and to identify what it is that must be present for peace to pertain, we can make five antinomies that deconstruct the sociological meaning of peace:

- Active versus Passive Peace
- Positive versus Negative Peace
- Social Transformation versus Conflict Transformation
- Peacebuilding versus Statebuilding
- Social Peace Process versus Political Peace Process.

The five antinomies of peace

It is hard to oppose the idea of peace. People may disagree with the settlement that brings it about, but the idea of peace has such universal appeal that it is most people's ideal. But the commitment to peace and the abstinence from war can be so passive as to be meaningless; peace can be on people's lips but not part of their daily practices, and its substance be empty and vacuous. Active peacebuilding turns peace from an ideal into an everyday life practice. If passive peace leads to any action at all, its first object is to change the other to make them acceptable. The first object of active peacebuilding, however, is to change oneself, and only then rebuild relationships with the other.

The famous distinction made by Johan Galtung (1969) between positive and negative peace is useful for further expanding the meaning of the term. Negative peace occurs when the violence ends. It can be a temporary halt, as with ceasefires, or a settlement that aims for more permanent ending. Positive peace is much more ambitious by trying to realise social justice, fairness in social, political and economic relations, redistributive justice in the allocation of scarce resources, the ending of human rights abuses, and democratic representation in politics and in the law. Active peacebuilding thus is not just about relationship building with the other through everyday life acts of peacebuilding, but a commitment to change the structural causes of the violence in the first place. This is a political goal that takes active peace well beyond philosophical ideals. And it implicates the state.

Inasmuch as this philosophical commitment to the ideal of peace is still a good thing and the ending of the killings is worthy in itself, the nomenclature of 'negative peace' sets the wrong tone about the concept of peace. I prefer to rename the distinction between negative and positive peace as the contrast between conflict transformation and social transformation. This makes clear that active peace has a personal goal to rebuild relationships with the erstwhile other in everyday life, simultaneously with the political goal to transform social relations to eliminate the structural causes of war and violence. Conflict transformation aims to end the killings; social transformation to end the injustice, inequality and unfairness that first provoked them.

Peace that delivers conflict transformation can involve no other social change than the ending of killings, leaving the structural disadvantages and injustices as a persistent threat to renewed violence. Despite this threat, dominant groups and regimes tend to favour conflict transformation, managing the risk of renewed conflict through various forms of social control of minority groups. Social control might temporarily bring about peacefulness, but it gives little substance to the meaning of peace. Subordinate groups prefer social transformation, wanting not just the absence of violence but the presence of social justice. The dominant group wants to maintain its dominance to avoid any loss of social privilege, so emphasises the social, political and economic benefits that come from an end to war without any attempt to address the need for social transformation.

The demand to maintain privilege is not true peace at all. Conflict transformation without social transformation will always make peace unstable. The level of social control of minority groups to manage the risk of renewed violence is itself destabilising, but the failure to eliminate structural disadvantage, discrimination and social injustice leaves what Galtung called 'structural violence', which is experienced as poverty, human rights abuses and distributive injustice. The process of democratisation from authoritarian regimes in Latin America has done little to empower the indigenous peoples, with power, wealth and prestige still remaining in the control of the descendants of European settlers, resulting in few democratic transitions there being completely stable. South Africa has done little to erode the legacy of apartheid, so while Black South Africans can exercise the franchise, the material lives of most have improved little. The complaint that they experience 'economic apartheid' has fuelled street demonstrations, student unrest and weakened the power of the African National Congress government, sustaining various opposition parties, including one ominously named The Economic Freedom Fighters, which, despite its name, is committed to political means. The liberation dream for second- and third-generation Black South Africans has become a nightmare (Adam and Moodley 2015).

In *Stride Toward Freedom* Martin Luther King Jr (1958) wrote that 'true peace is not merely the absence of tension: it is the presence of justice', which he later repeated in the famous letter from Birmingham Jail in 1963, and which is inscribed on the North Wall of his memorial stone in Washington DC. This reflects in the need for social transformation to move at the same pace as conflict transformation, a linking that also ennobles Lederach's (1999, 2005) concept of 'justpeace', a new noun that denotes the indivisibility of peace (the absence of violence) and justice (the presence of fair desserts). Without social justice there is what Lederach calls 'the justice gap'. Members of dominant groups see the justice gap as describing the absence of retributive justice for perpetrators of violence, the amnesties given to whom as an incentive to enter the negotiation process still rankles; members of subordinate groups see it as the absence of social change, the resistance to which amongst the dominant groups threatens peace.

A further antinomy that elaborates on what must be present in what Martin Luther King Jr calls 'true peace' is the distinction between peacebuilding and statebuilding. Statebuilding refers to the institutional reforms that strengthen the structures of governance after conflict, designed to eliminate problematic politics and introduce democracy. Weak states after war are problematic. They often continue the war economy that sustains warlords, corruption and pilfering of aid, they encourage anti-democratic spoiler groups that continue the war, use food and hunger as political leverages, and abuse human rights. Weak states are also sanctuaries for international terror groups who conceal themselves in the chaos to continue their terror campaigns. Weak states can do

UNDERSTANDING WHAT PEACE MEANS SOCIOLOGICALLY 27

little to enhance the sense of flourishing that peace enables for the victims of war. Statebuilding is therefore important to avoid the problems of weak states. Statebuilding is reflected in institutional reform of the structures of governance, including of parliamentary institutions, voting systems, the police and security forces, institutions of civil administration like the civil service, and the creation of new institutions to monitor the effectiveness of governance reforms, such as equality commissions, human rights commissions, commissions for victims' rights, commissions for the protection of women and children, and so forth.

It is naïve to assume, however, that once problematic politics is addressed through statebuilding, erstwhile enemies will develop moral sensibility and naturally come to live in tolerance with each other. The rebuilding of broken relationships, the restoration of trust, developing resilience in local communities and civil society, and the elimination of fear require much more than effective statebuilding. Institutional reform done at the neglect of societal healing will result only in a cold peace: where people no longer kill one another but still live in separate social worlds. They are kept apart by the normal outworkings of social institutions that effortlessly reproduce separateness through segregated marriage patterns, segregated friendship and kinship networks, separate residential choices, and separate schooling, work and leisure, all of which keep aflame the social cleavages of 'race', ethnicity, religion, language, culture and colonisation in which past conflict was embedded. Some cleavages are maintained through law (as was apartheid and Nazism), and some by physical force that imposes segregation (as on the West Bank, and in Balkan ethnic cleansing), but some are kept alive symbolically *after* the peace has been won by social structures that reproduce social separateness. This happens in post-apartheid South Africa and in post-Good Friday Agreement Northern Ireland, resulting in a cold peace.

If statebuilding is about institutional reform to the structures of governance, peacebuilding is about reform of the very social institutions that reproduce mutually antagonistic identity formations, divided communities, weak civil societies and community development, and which promote fear, mistrust, polarisation, and the 'othering' of those deemed 'not one of us'. Peacebuilding warms up peace by forms of societal healing that change the social structure in which division is routinely reproduced.

28   ADVANCED INTRODUCTION TO THE SOCIOLOGY OF PEACE PROCESSES

This brings us to the last antinomy between social peace processes and political peace processes. A peace process is commonly thought to describe the political negotiations that bring an end to the war. This reinforces the sense that they are political processes. There is another reason why they are assumed to be political. As described here, they are commanded over by politicians, political parties and governments, usually assisted by professional conflict resolution experts rather than members of the affected communities, and the emphasis is upon resolving problematic politics through statebuilding. I refer to this as the political peace process. Statebuilding does not, however, deliver peacebuilding. South Africa's 'new rainbow nation' disappeared with the first hard rains, as did Sri Lanka's 'one Sri Lanka' identity. And 23 years after signing the Good Friday Agreement in Northern Ireland, we still await the implementation of some of its equality agenda. Peacebuilding needs a dedicated strategy of social structural reform that realises societal healing, which involves emotional and financial investment as generous as that directed to the shiny buildings that house the new institutions of governance.

The social peace process addresses at its core the problem of societal healing through peacebuilding. I have written many times that the social peace process is too important to be left to politicians. The social peace process is commanded over by civil society. This means by women's groups, youth groups, churches, trade unions, the universities, businesses, local regeneration and community development groups; by people who are active peacebuilders as referred to earlier, people dedicated not just to rebuilding personal relationships with the other, but to a life's vocation of peace that is committed to social transformation and social structural reform.

There is another problem arising from the tension between the social and political peace processes. They operate on different time frames. Governance structures and institutions can be quickly devised and implemented. Statebuilding in the political peace process can advance quickly, if not necessarily always successfully. Foreign aid money can bolster weak economies rapidly and diminish the power of warlords that perpetuate war economies, and new voting systems can result quickly in fairer elections. This compressed time frame is partly the reason why peace processes can be wrongly perceived to have reached their conclusion when the new institutions are up and running. There is, of course, public awareness that new governance structures take time to institutionalise and become embedded, but this is seen as just a matter of time. Institutions carry their own institutionalisation in time.

Societal healing, however, has to operate on a much longer time frame. This is sometimes a source of great frustration, as people get exasperated when longstanding conflicts erupt at flashpoints or when societies emerging from conflict seem not to have learned the lessons of the past. The social peace process, however, is of long duration. This is one of the reasons why institutional reform in the political peace process can be seen to be progressing well, while interpersonal antagonisms and group conflicts continue, making societal healing seem as far away as ever. This is Northern Ireland's conundrum.

Two things follow from these temporal considerations. Social peace processes require patience; they also demand sustained attention, long after the large-scale killing has stopped. Patience, however, is another casualty of peace. Time frames of expectation are very short, as people want peace on their terms and want it now. Forgiveness, truth, reintegration and healing, however, are for the long term; reconciliation proceeds slowly and often stumbles. The contradiction is plain. On the one hand, the social peace process presents people with challenges that make it difficult to embrace former enemies, while conversely, people get frustrated and exasperated when old resentments and divisions resurface. This is the paradox of social peace processes.

So, what, sociologically, is peace?

To understand what a sociological definition of peace involves, we must link back to debates in Chapter 2 about the moral sensibility in which recent sociological engagements with war and peace have been framed. The sociological definition of peace developed here sees it as the restoration of social solidarity after conflict. This sense of social togetherness, however, requires the restoration of sociability, of living together in tolerance despite difference. Social solidarity and sociability are mediated, however, by social justice. Continued social *in*justice stymies the restoration of sociability amongst erstwhile enemies and inhibits the development of senses of social solidarity. This alliteration of solidarity, sociability and social justice requires us to rethink what we mean by peace. As emphasised in this chapter, this means that peace is more than conflict transformation, an ending of violence; it requires social transformation.

The absence of social transformation bedevils peace processes and threatens the political gains made as a result of conflict transformation. Social justice thus becomes the key to peace after conflict, reflected in Lederach's use of the new noun 'justpeace'.

A minimalist definition of peace is that it is the absence of war. A sociological definition is maximalist, in making it the presence of active and positive peace, committed to social transformation and to peacebuilding, occurring within a social peace process that emphasises societal healing through reform to the social structure.

However, while sociology provides us with a fuller description of the meaning of peace than hitherto, the definition says little about the process involved in bringing it about or the types of peace processes that exist. Sociology makes an invaluable contribution here as well.

What is a peace process?

Peace processes are the transitions societies make from communal violence to relative non-violence, with the intention to restore peace, that is, to achieve social solidarity, sociability and social justice. Three points are worth making at the outset. First, the threat of violence is rarely fully eliminated in the transition, and these societies have to balance the maintenance of peace with the management of the risks to renewed violence. These aims can work against each other in the process and the transition from violence is relative; they are never fully 'post-violence societies' (Brewer 2010: 19). Second, the transition from communal violence is a process of long duration, involving a cycle of policy initiatives, reforms to institutions, changes to social relations within the social structure, intra-personal change to active peacebuilding and interpersonal growth in cross-communal social relationships. It is a precarious journey, with ups and downs, highs and lows, that requires the level of commitment and resources once found to sustain the war. Third, people's enthusiasm for the process can wane; and not just amongst its opponents. Disappointed expectations at the pace of the process amongst enthusiasts are as damaging to it as opposition from those who rail against it. Peace processes are thus inherently fragile. These prosaic observations are the backcloth to what is the main contribution of the sociological imagination to understanding peace processes. This is its deconstruction of the types of transition involved in peace processes (what follows is a modern reworking of Brewer 2010: 19–28, 2013c: 164–5, from where further details can be found).

A sociological typology of peace processes

Peace processes come in three forms, and for the sake of alliteration, I call them conquest (via a victor's peace), cartography (with peace via partition), and compromise (with peace via a mutually agreed second preference settlement). They cohere around three axes:

- Relational distance–closeness
- Spatial separation–territorial integrity
- Cultural capital–cultural annihilation.

Relational distance–closeness refers to the extent to which former enemies share common values (in that belligerents can fight over small or large differences). The greater the relational distance, the more likely it is that the lines of fissure that provoked the conflict endure into the peace process, and ways have to be found to either eradicate them or reproduce them in non-violent ways. The smallness of the degree of asserted difference between the warring factions is in inverse proportion to their relational closeness, so societal healing in a peace process is facilitated by a nation rebuilding project after conflict based around relational closeness. Spatial separation–territorial integrity refers to the degree to which former belligerents continue to share common land and nationhood. The greater the spatial separation, the more likely it is that the lines of fissure that provoked the conflict can be managed by various forms of regional devolution, or even partition. Full territorial integrity, on the other hand, ensures the continuance of the national entity within which, or over which, former belligerents went to war. In these circumstances, the peace process has to manage the legacy of neighbour killing neighbour. Cultural capital–cultural annihilation addresses the level of cultural capital possessed by the various warring factions. The greater their level of cultural capital, the more powerful factions become in the negotiation process to end the war, empowering their voice and interests in any settlement. The less cultural capital they possess, the easier it becomes to subjugate them to a process of cultural annihilation, which does not necessarily imply physical eradication through genocide but the stripping away of cultural and other resources for resistance. Annihilated cultures – Australian

32   ADVANCED INTRODUCTION TO THE SOCIOLOGY OF PEACE PROCESSES

indigenous peoples, North and South American indigenous Indians, South African Hottentots – survive but furnish members with little material or symbolic capital to resist their colonial dispossession.

These axes intersect (Figure 3.1) in ways that confer three main types of peace process. The first is conquest, where a victor's peace terminates the conflict.

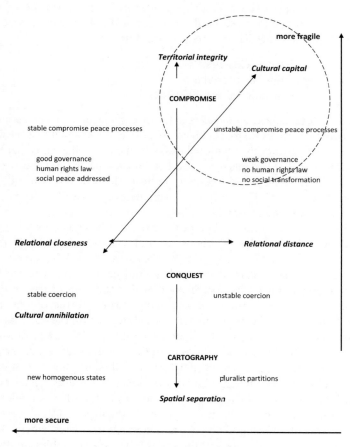

Figure 3.1   Types of peace process

UNDERSTANDING WHAT PEACE MEANS SOCIOLOGICALLY   33

It realises what was referred to earlier as negative peace, a form of conflict transformation in which the war ends by victory for one set of belligerents, who have no incentive to implement a fuller and more flourishing form of social peace process. Instead, the vanquished can be subjected to cultural annihilation, experiencing a double victimhood, with the second form of injury being to the group's very identity and survival. Where the defeated retain cultural capital, in the form of labour power, third-party international support and extensive diaspora networks, cultural annihilation is never complete and the risk of renewed conflict is high, if not always immediate. A victor's peace is fragile wherever the defeated retain cultural capital. A victor's peace is consolidated only by means of oppressive social control of the defeated and by their cultural annihilation with a level of repression that hardly deserves the name peace. Nonetheless, a victor's peace won settler groups their stability after colonial dispossession, and it sees Sinhalese communities prosper in modern Sri Lanka after the defeat of Tamil insurgents.

Cartography delivers peace through partition, with redrawn national boundaries, new states and devolved regions used to isolate and separate the groups that reflect contested social cleavages. Peace through partition is easier where former belligerents are separated spatially and have little or no relational closeness. While partition and federal devolution impugn the territorial integrity of the nation state, spatial separation can be preferred as a type of peace process, since it can be used to 'purify' the ethnic, racial, religious or linguistic identity of the new territory, ridding it of competing identities. Cartography thus not only redraws the territorial map; it reshapes the symbolic map. Peace via partition, however, is not always stable. Internal civil conflicts can be transformed into conflict rivalries between the new nation states, such as between India and Pakistan, and partition offers a new provocation to conflict, merely delaying the eruption of violence later around opposition to it, such as in Ireland. Furthermore, peace through partition is not possible where the conflict has no geographical basis, where it involves complex social cleavages that are not linked to territorial claims, and where divisions of territory are not possible because of geography and landscape.

Compromise is a peace process that delivers a second preference negotiated settlement, in which groups forego their first option for a mutually agreed second best. It is premised on recognising there is a military stalemate in which victory is not possible for any party or group, and first preferences are abandoned in order to bring the unwinnable conflict to an end. Mutually agreed settlements offer some form of closure to the conflict and a new beginning. Compromise peace processes thus exist at the interface of the past and the future. They are more stable where there is relational closeness between the erstwhile enemies, where the lines of fissure conceal fewer differences than the conflict would suggest, and where the differences over which people fought do not touch what Rex (1981: 8) called people's 'sense of ultimate values'. They are also more stable where spatial separation is impracticable, persuading people to confront the choice of either finding ways of learning to live together in tolerance or continue with the war. This is, in effect, a Hobson's Choice – no choice at all – for peace is the only option with military stalemates.

Compromise peace processes are unstable where there is relational difference, in that groups share territory but inhabit different social worlds, where levels of cultural capital are unequal between the groups, allowing power differences to be maintained and for dominant groups to challenge their loss of privilege, and when some parties to the conflict renege on the terms of the settlement, try to renegotiate it, or remain loyal to first preferences. Compromise peace processes can therefore be fragile. 'Peace', sociologically understood, can be empty enough in these circumstances. The demands of the social peace process can go unmet with little societal healing, the degree of social transformation involved to realise 'justpeace' can be limited, and peacebuilding can be neglected in favour of statebuilding.

The three analytical axes that successfully distinguish between types of peace process clearly identify compromise peace processes to be the most preferable, but also the most difficult. This type epitomises what is commonly thought of as a peace process, with parties coming together to negotiate a settlement in which no first preference wins, but all win with a second-best preference deal. It presents sociology with an interesting challenge however, for in the context of territorial integrity, relational distance and continued but unequal cultural capital, the transition from war to peace with compromise peace processes is the most difficult to manage. This challenge, however, is also sociology's opportunity, for the discipline offers an intellectual lens through which to identify the issues involved in managing compromise peace processes, the strengths and weaknesses of this type, as well as the new ideas and concepts it brings to such an analysis.

Compromise peace processes

Learning to live together in tolerance after conflict within a compromise peace process, when partition does not separate people territorially or coercion culturally annihilate them, defines the problem of moral sensibility that provoked the emergence of sociology in the first place, and which motivated sociology's later interest in new forms of war and peace. Issues that promote or inhibit moral sensibility in compromise peace processes are therefore at the kernel of their success or failure.

Sociology adds less to our understanding of the negotiation process that brings about the second preference settlement, which is based on skills-based conflict mediation, but it has a great deal to contribute to understanding the issues that need to be managed to make them successful. We have already established the importance of the five antinomies of peace that presuppose an expansive view of peace. These antinomies capture that the negotiated settlement that delivers the compromise second preference deal is never the end of peacemaking, for accords mostly leave unresolved the processes for societal healing in the social peace process.

The sorts of actions that focus the social peace process include truth and reconciliation procedures, forgiveness and atonement strategies, policies that facilitate and encourage public tolerance and compromise, new forms of memory work, memorialisation and remembering, public apologies, forgiveness strategies, new cultural symbols, such as national flags, anthems and the like, language acts that recognise minority rights, and the reassessment and re-evaluation of identity. In conflict societies where social inequality is high and which was itself part of the cause of conflict, as occurs often in settler and divided societies and with wars of decolonisation, societal healing is greatly assisted by policies of social redistribution, for people's senses of justice are narrowed to reflect their experiences of inequality; the demand for justice is a surrogate for demands for social redistribution (on competing notions of justice in post-conflict settings, see Sen 1999; Wolterstorff 2008, 2013). When equivalence occurs between justice as human rights and justice as socio-economic redistribution, the social peace process is helped as much by policies that eliminate inequality as prevention of human rights abuses. Abject failure in social transformation can lead to new outbreaks of conflict.

On top of these considerations, however, there are many issues that sociology illuminates which are critical to the consolidation of the mutually agreed second preference peace process. Where the pace of transformation is slow, a compromise peace process can lose its energy and positive momentum. This loss of momentum can reflect, amongst other things, in public bickering over the meaning of the terms of the initial peace settlement, the growth of anti-agreement sentiment amongst its opponents, frustration and desperation amongst its supporters at the lack of progress, and slowness, hesitancy and dissimulation amongst those responsible for making the agreement work. This can allow anti-agreement forces to grow by using a series of legacy issues as the means to mobilise anti-agreement sentiment, rekindling support for first preferences.

The importance of legacy issues in compromise peace processes is not coincidental. Legacy issues emerge as a natural part of compromise peace processes, since the problem of the past is inherent to the process of conflict transformation itself. No matter how successful the introduction of new governance structures and the institutional reform of politics through statebuilding, compromise peace processes are left with a series of legacy issues that are important to reconciliation and healing in society and, if not adequately addressed, can destabilise the political gains and slow the process of societal healing. There is no way of avoiding or side-lining these legacy issues, since they emerge inevitably in the course of a peace process at the point when memory of the violence recedes and debate about the morality of the conflict supersedes that about the conflict itself.

Legacy issues concern specific policy questions like amnesty for former combatants and the range of victim and survivor policies, but also more broad matters like dealing with the past, and the meaning of values like tolerance, truth, mercy, justice and forgiveness. These legacy issues rarely surface in the immediate aftermath of a negotiated settlement for the euphoria and expectations at the ending of conflict side-lines them. The paradox of legacy issues is that they emerge only sometime later, in the long and difficult process of learning to live together once the violence is largely over, when people's expectations of change have been disappointed or are re-evaluated in the light of experience, and the compromise peace process seems to bounce along at the bottom. This is precisely when the compromise peace process is at its lowest ebb, a point when people come to realise that learning to live together is not automatic and does not follow naturally once the violence has ended. Therefore, legacy issues seem to supporters of the peace process only to make it worse, while to opponents of the peace settlement, legacy issues epitomise the fraudulence of the whole process.

In particular, compromise peace processes can experience contestation over the morality of the conflict, whether or not it was justified, and for what purpose it was fought. With the political arrangements in the political peace process bedding in, even if only slowly, contestation can focus on the morality of the violence. These debates can threaten the compromise deal. Three observations are worth making here that are relevant to the problem of moral sensibility in compromise peace processes. First, this is a debate about the legacy of the past, not about what a peaceful, shared future might look like. The past has become the arbiter of the future. People living with a compromise peace process can argue about the morality of the conflict, not about the moral imagination, as Lederach (2005) puts it, needed to re-envision a shared society in the future. Second, these legacy issues can be openly exploited to focus mobilisation against the political peace process, used strategically by opponents to try to reverse political gains. Third, in this maelstrom of anti-agreement mobilisation, there can be a downwardly spiralling cycle of moral recalibration that is both counter-productive to progress in the social peace process and is morally reprehensible.

I have argued elsewhere that some societies with compromise peace processes have 'pathological memory cultures' that extenuate the obsession with the past (Brewer 2020, 2021b), where life is experienced largely through the past and society is thought thus to change little despite the peace. Memory almost becomes morbid in these pathological memory cultures. This argument draws on the familiar criticisms of the collective memory literature, which claims that collective memories can enslave rather than liberate humankind (Rieff 2016: 62), lead to abuses of memory (Berliner 2005; Todorov 2003), turn memorialisation sacred (Misztal 2004), and lead to what Rieff dismissively characterises as the fascist-like homage to 'the duty of memory' (2016: 63) and the 'dictatorship of nostalgia' (2016: 93).

While it is a general complaint of collective memory studies that memory can be turned into an obsession, there are at least two conditions under which compromise peace processes are particularly prone to develop

38   ADVANCED INTRODUCTION TO THE SOCIOLOGY OF PEACE PROCESSES

pathological memory cultures. The first is where conservative forms of the Abrahamic faiths dominate. In such circumstances orthodox and traditional religious interpretations invoke an unbroken continuity with ancient times, predisposing covenantal ideas and a 'Chosen People' status, preaching an elective affinity between religion, identity and the land, and having conservative forms of religious culture. It is no coincidence that covenantal theology, Chosen People status and the elision of territory, religion and identity feature in a great number of memory conflicts (Akenson 1992; Brewer and Higgins 1998), with Christ appropriated to be on competing sides at the same time (Elliott 2009). Some religious cultures thus bear heavily upon societal healing in negative ways.

The second condition that predisposes pathological memory cultures is when the transition is problematic or challenged, with groups mistrusting the carefully negotiated second preference peace agreement and remaining loyal to mutually exclusive first preferences. In peace processes where there is no clear winner, erstwhile enemies are better able to sustain their discordant memories and use memory to perpetuate division. Processes of cultural reproduction sustain and disseminate the ancient cleavages and divisions, weakening and slowing the social peace process; relationships remain broken, conflict journalism abounds, communities remain divided, and wounds are deliberately kept open. Injury and offence are hung onto tenaciously as part of their zero-sum identity and the present is thought to have enduring continuity with the past. Erstwhile enemies can share different senses of the past and have little sense of a shared future. People can transfer the physical war of the past into a culture war that involves conflict over, amongst other things, memory, memory symbols and symbolic representations of the past.

Pathological memory cultures under these conditions tend to sustain divided moral frameworks that negatively affect the recreation of moral sensibility in compromise peace processes. Moral recalibration downwards reflects in selective moral condemnation of the past, such as in the way respective communities honour their own combatants but criticise the 'other community' for honouring theirs, and in demands for amnesty for one's own ex-combatants, but not for all. Selective moralisation is manifest also in the strident assertion of the right to one's own cultural practices but the unwillingness to accept the cultural practices of the 'other'.

This selective moral condemnation can stoop so low as to distort the meaning of justice in 'justpeace'. Justice is one of the key principles on which to build compromise peace processes; not the only one – there is also the need for fairness, equality of opportunity, hope, social betterment, and the alleviation of human need and want – but justice is amongst the capstones. However, justice is backward looking as much as forward looking; it is about dealing with past *in*justices as well as improving justice in the future. Inasmuch as justice is about the past as well as the future, justice is much broader than merely its criminal applications. Justice is not just about prosecuting past criminal wrongs; it is about ensuring that past wrongs are not repeated. And the wrongs that need to be avoided are not only criminal acts; they are all previous social, political, cultural and economic practices which ended up in people being treated unfairly, unjustly as second-class citizens, and without regard to their common dignity as human beings. With this approach, justice is truly blind. All people are of equal worth. All people have equal dignity. All people should be treated fairly. All people deserve equal justice. No one is above the law, and no one deserves less justice than another. There are no second-class citizens. Justice, however, can also be one-eyed.

Justice is one-eyed when only some people's rights to justice are accorded privilege, or when some people's injustices get attention, and the injustices of others are forgotten. Justice is one-eyed when we pursue only some people's past wrongs, or only some kinds of past wrongs and not others. Justice has to be truly blind, in the sense of universally applied, if it is to be the capstone for a compromise peace process. One-eyed justice ends up with an unjust form of justice, for it ends up pursuing past wrongs selectively. Justice that is not truly blind is no justice at all.

Compromise peace processes have a tendency to use selective moral condemnation, because people locate the various problems arising from the legacy of the conflict within different and competing moral frameworks that can persist despite the peace settlement. Where there is no shared peace vocation, no shared moral vision as to what peace means and what it might deliver for their grandchildren, and no common value orientation promoted by the shared commitment to the idea of peace, the same polarised moral frameworks can survive, and which helped to shape the conflict in the first place. There can be a complete moral vacuum when it comes to imagining what a shared, peaceful future might look like.

40 ADVANCED INTRODUCTION TO THE SOCIOLOGY OF PEACE PROCESSES

This moral vacuum reflects in three ways. The first is the use of victim hierarchy in which one's own community is said to have suffered the most, with the 'other' community's ex-combatants being the more heinous. The second is the use of blaming strategies in which the 'other' community's ex-combatants are always the ones with the primary responsibility for the conflict and are the ones provoking renewed violence. The third is the avoidance of acknowledgement – the absence of internal reflexivity within people and organisations – in which they reflect on their own acts of commission or acts of omission, during both the conflict and the peace. In this way, some people in compromise peace processes ask of others what they refuse to do themselves. Selective moral condemnation can be a morally corrupting practice, leading to fruitless debates about who killed more, who suffered more and who was the more heinous. It is morally repugnant to respect some victims over others, to condemn some killings and not all, to demand some are held to account but not others, and to engage in a sectarian headcount of who killed the least (or the most). This sort of moral recalibration downwards has very negative consequences for the likelihood of progress in the social peace process.

These partisan moral condemnations particularly affect the treatment of two constituencies that are problematic for compromise peace processes, ex-combatants and victims. These are not necessarily separate categories (Jankowitz 2018) but there is an interesting sociology around both groups. In what I have described elsewhere as the martyr–hero–demon syndrome (Brewer 2021a, 2021c) through which ex-combatants are sanctified or vilified, the processes through which they are socially constructed as martyrs, heroes or demons are deeply sociological. Some cultures, for example, tend to valorise the tradition of the long dead (Ignatieff 1998), making the burden of self-sacrifice, spilled blood and martyrdom of previous generations literally a dead weight on the future. Martyrs, however, are socially constructed to speak to the present, not the past. They embolden current combatants, and refresh recruitment with the reassurance that sacrifice is never forgotten, in poetry, song, storytelling and various rituals of commemoration. Martyrs tend to keep the conflict alive, always in memory and sometimes in practice by sustaining others' commitment to first preferences.

An interesting sociological question is why martyrdom is constructed for some combatants and not for others. Combatants' role in life and death helps in the social construction of martyrdom. Sometimes this is explained by their high social status in life; sometimes the iconic manner of their death. Dirk Moses (2021), for example, refers to Jewish martyrs as those sacrificed as tokens for the group, notably in the Holocaust, although this applies to all members of ethnic groups killed in genocide. He also emphasises the motives of the murderer in the construction of martyrs, seeing groundless killings of innocents as turning victims into martyrs. Material culture can make some deaths notorious, captured on film, in photographs, reproduced in murals and oral traditions to reinforce their power to speak to the present. The manner of death can turn martyrs into symbols of political protest and become symbolic weapons. Martyrdom is thus sociologically constructed in large part by the use to which the iconic status can be put in the present. As I have argued before (Brewer 2021c: 24–5), peace processes settled by second preference deals do not necessarily change people's private personal feelings towards killers, even if in public they practise tolerance, so the true measure of societal healing is when people no longer use mutually exclusive moral frameworks to demonise opposing perpetrators, or hero worship their own.

Another constituency whose treatment is critical to the development of moral sensibility in compromise peace processes is victims. Again, deeply sociological processes affect their treatment. Behind every dreadful experience of victimhood there is a subsequent process of social construction that distorts those experiences and uses them for other purposes (Brewer et al. 2018: 26–34). Victims do not socially construct injuries; it is the moral category of 'victim' that is socially constructed. Who counts as a victim (or ex-combatant) is largely determined after the conflict as legacy issues dominate the public sphere, meaning only some victims matter. Additional layers of meaning are given to victimhood by the press, politicians, religious figures, cultural commentators and so on, seeing only some victims as 'true victims' and 'innocent victims'. People can be the 'wrong' victim, inasmuch as they do not fit the other's social construction of the 'ideal' victim. Certain atrocities become notorious in the process of social construction, bestowing status on victims, while others are ignored. What I have called 'preferred victims' are canonised, while 'wrong victims' are forgotten (Brewer et al. 2018: 38–9). As I have argued, this turns some victims almost into celebrities (or martyrs if they died), whose experiences and celebrity-like status are exploited for ulterior purpose (Brewer et al. 2018: 30). Most victims do not collude in the manufacture of this celebrity-like status, although some do.

42   ADVANCED INTRODUCTION TO THE SOCIOLOGY OF PEACE PROCESSES

The social construction of victimhood is significantly impacted by the cultural tropes through which victims are discussed in the public sphere in compromise peace processes (for elaboration of these tropes in Northern Ireland, South Africa and Sri Lanka, see Brewer et al. 2018: 41–4). These tropes are widely circulated in popular culture, everyday life, in the mass media, and in political discourse. They offer standardised scripts and cultural frames through which to understand and talk about victimhood. They disempower victims because they strip victims of their own voice, such that victims are heard only through the cultural tropes that others use to talk about victimhood.

When victims' voices are captured directly, not filtered through cultural tropes, their emotional landscape is sociologically profound. In research undertaken on first-generation victims in Northern Ireland, South Africa and Sri Lanka (Brewer, Hayes and Teeney 2018; Brewer et al. 2018), for example, it was apparent that very few had 'victim identities' which locked them into the moment of their victimhood and froze them in time and identity. They tended to see themselves as survivors, on a path to post-traumatic growth, in which their emotional landscape reflected emotional behaviours and forms of talk around hope, forgiveness, compromise and empathy towards the other. This gives sociology the opportunity to develop a sociology of compromise (Brewer, Hayes and Teeney 2018), a sociology of forgiveness (Brewer 2010: 133–9, 2018b: 246–9), a sociology of hope (Brewer 2010: 125–31, 2018b: 249–51), and a sociology of anger (Brewer 2018b: 243–4), amongst other things. This is the basis of the claim that first-generation victims can be 'moral beacons', holding up a light for the rest of society to follow in compromise peace processes (see also Brewer and Hayes, 2011b).

Conclusion

The implication of my argument here is that the problems faced by compromise peace processes in managing the social peace process are as much moral as political. Moral sensibility can reverse any negative moral recalibration by re-envisioning peace, by recommitting the society to a peace vocation, and by developing a value orientation that shapes a new moral imagination. Compromise peace processes can experience a moral vacuum that needs to be replenished, not with the same old divided and competing moral frameworks that shaped the conflict in the past, but infilled with an embracing, uplifting, hope-inspiring vision of peace. That is, with a moral sensibility that assists people in learning to live together in tolerance after conflict. Exploring the recreation of moral sensibility in compromise peace processes offers sociology the opportunity to contribute new ideas and concepts to the field.

A sociological definition of peace and the associated typology of peace processes offer a new empirical research agenda for the study of compromise peace processes. As highlighted in this chapter, sociology opens the field up to an analysis of societal healing in the social peace process, and how this is impacted by a political economy of decolonisation, class and social justice. Sociology alerts us to the practice of compromise in interpersonal relations; to victims' emotions like anger, forgiveness, hope, empathy and mercy; to the management of cultural trauma; to the moral claims to legitimacy made by ex-combatants that move the debate about participation in conflict beyond hyper-masculinity; to the social construction of the moral categories of 'combatant' and 'victim'; to the social manufacture of cultural tropes that distort the moral frameworks for properly understanding victims and ex-combatants, resulting in the misleading martyr–hero–demon syndrome; to problems like bystander guilt and the unforgivingness of some religious cultures; of the problems around pathological memory cultures that deform the past, and thus alerting us to the new forms of memory work needed to overcome the dismembering of history in pathological memory cultures, which elsewhere I have called 'remembering forwards' (Brewer 2020); to the potential for peace journalism to re-envision a shared future; to the role of civil society in garnering the social peace process; to the potential for religious peacebuilding (Brewer, Higgins and Teeney 2011), everyday life peacebuilding (Brewer et al. 2018), and much, much more. Some of these new concepts and ideas are elaborated in the following chapters.

4 The sociology of compromise after conflict

Introduction

This chapter briefly introduces one of the new ideas that a sociology of peace processes announces, namely intersubjective or social compromise (these ideas are elaborated in Brewer 2018b, 2018c). Political deals that are negotiated compromises have long interested international relations specialists, and so-called 'rotten' ones that consolidate human indignity and injustice have concerned ethicists (Margalit 2010). The connection between compromise in politics and democracy is also a long concern (for a recent treatment, see Baume and Novak 2020). And solipsistic considerations about compromises *within* the self have interested political theorists (Leopora 2012; Leopora and Goodin 2013). The sociology of compromise, however, addresses compromise at the interpersonal level between people who have to learn to live together in tolerance after conflict, in what we can call social compromise.

After outlining the features of the concept and its sociological dynamics, the chapter ends by demonstrating the contribution social compromise makes to moral sensibility and the restoration of sociability after conflict. I argue that the social practice of compromise in the public sphere amongst first-generation victims is deeply embedded in the understanding they have of their own ethical responsibilities arising from their victimhood. Victimhood obligates its own ethical response, which most first-generation victims express as an obligation to 'get along' with one another for the sake of the future, which I have termed a 'relational' rather than 'subjective' ethic. In short, the social practice of compromise carries its own ethical practices, allowing society to reproduce itself after conflict. The social practice of compromise thus becomes one of the key practices for sociability after conflict, premised on this relational ethic of 'getting along'. This argument highlights how thoroughly sociological the concept is, and how relevant a consideration of compromise is to the sociological definition of peace advanced in Chapter 2. Compromise links to the practice of moral sensibility after conflict and thus to the development of sociability as the fulcrum of the social peace process.

A sociological approach to compromise

Compromise is seen as a moral imperative in late modernity (Walker 2006), part of the 'moral turn' in peace and humanitarian studies (a phrase used in Brewer et al. 2017). Ethical approaches to the political task of post-conflict reconstruction thus abound. Philpott (2012) defined what he called the ethic of political reconciliation, Shriver (1995) the ethic of political forgiveness, which he referred to as an ethic for former enemies, and Blustein (2014) to the ethic of remembrance. The point about ethical systems is that they refer simultaneously to the personal emotional interiority of the practitioner, in that they attend to their senses of trauma (Alexander 2012), vulnerability (Misztal 2011a; Turner 2006) and need for human dignity (Margalit 2010; Wolterstorff 2008), while at the same time describe cultural and normative practices that are social and collective. Ethical standards thus go to shape whole societies as much as individual behaviour. The ethical imperative to practise compromise in society and in interpersonal behaviour does not, however, make compromise any easier to understand or define. The prevalence of the term in lay discourse and in popular culture, along with those of tolerance, reconciliation and forgiveness, suggests there is a need for sociology to begin to problematise what compromise means sociologically.

Elsewhere I have defined social compromise after conflict sociologically as the reciprocal practice of tolerance and civility towards former protagonists in the public sphere, involving an act of will, to avoid behaving and talking in public space in the ways that people's emotions in the private sphere would normally dictate, thereby assisting people to keep to their reciprocal obligations to tolerance (Brewer 2018c: 9). Two features of this definition stand out. First, compromise after conflict works through moral sensibility but is different from it. There is a long-established philosophical debate about civility and toleration as key elements of moral sensibility, in which toleration is rendered as discrete practices within the public sphere that assists democratic dialogue (O'Neill 1993), with civility portrayed as the *exercise* of tolerance in the face of deep disagreement (Calhoun 2000: 256). While compromise is outworked through moral sensibility, it is not equivalent to it. Moral sensibility after conflict is premised first on the ability to compromise, such that compromise makes moral sensibility possible. A sociological approach to compromise is thus less concerned with clarifying the virtues that comprise moral sensibility (an approach taken by Ignatieff 2017) than specifying the interpersonal and social structural conditions under which compromise allows moral sensibility to flourish.

Second, this definition renders compromise into a social practice. In sociology, the term social practice is treated almost as an equivalent to social action, describing forms of relationships, activities and discursive strategies that are normative. Normative is meant in both its sociological senses: something that is based on norms (that is, grounded in actual values, beliefs and behaviours) and is also socially desirable (that is, it has virtue attached to it as an ideal). Sociologically, therefore, social practices constitute the norms, values, habits and behaviours that describe the regular patterns of social life (the way of living together and talking to one another as practised in society) and the aspirational ideals on which social life ought to be lived (the virtuous way to practise living together and talking to one another in society). In sociology, therefore, social practices are forms of social relationships that reproduce society, either as it is mundanely practised (made into the norm) or idealised into something better (made normative).

In this definition, compromise is a social practice that involves performing the ritualised behaviours and forms of talk that promote moral sensibility, tolerance and civility towards former protagonists in the public sphere so that people can keep to the reciprocal obligations that mark the compromise. It provides what C. Wright Mills (1940) once called a 'vocabulary of motives' that institutionalise ways of expressing emotions. Compromise is both a norm (capable of being practised) and normative (virtuous as an ideal). This draws on two sets of mainstream sociological ideas: the sociology of emotions, which points to the distinction between feelings and their enactment in behaviour, and which illustrates people's capacity to perform actions and talk contrary to how they feel, enabling

Emotions as performed behaviour

In one of the best discussions of emotions in transitional justice by a sociologist, Elster (2004) argued that emotions induce senses of urgency and impatience that short-circuit people's usual prudence, but these are momentary. However, while emotions have a short shelf life, people subject to them lack any anticipation that these feelings will decay: we expect to continue to feel what our emotions tell us at the moment of their experience. In this respect, people's emotions transcend their momentariness and can be separated from raw feelings. Feelings and behaviour are distinct. Emotionally induced urgency, impatience and intensity can inflame feelings within us that result in action that is thought of as unavoidable, yet these feelings need not be enacted; the behaviour is entirely avoidable. We may choose (or not be able) to act out the emotions we feel at the moment of their experience, for while all emotions have behaviours and forms of talk related to them, these action tendencies are not culturally or genetically encoded and can be overruled.

The action tendencies associated with particular emotional feelings are performative behaviours (actions that are performed, behaviourally and linguistically, according to the socially learned scripts by which emotion work is conventionally done and talked about). Emotions are artful in two senses therefore, in that the feelings are constructed in their performance and this performance can be uncoupled from what is actually being felt. The latter may occur because we may either lack any of the feelings associated with the ritualised behaviour we are enacting and talking (we are pretending an emotion) or we are performing behaviours and talking entirely contrary to how we feel (we are disguising an emotion). The social practices and normative structures we experience as constraints and which prevent us from acting out our feelings of the moment, can be used to persuade us to act and talk in ways opposite to our momentary emotional response, whether for individual reasons, like conscience or personal gain, or social and cultural pressure and legal sanction.

48   ADVANCED INTRODUCTION TO THE SOCIOLOGY OF PEACE PROCESSES

There is a further lesson from the sociology of emotions. Emotions are modulated by social relations (Elster 2004: 217). They can be kept vivid or moderated by our social networks, which can assist in the reinforcement of feelings and sustain the patterns of action and forms of talk they enact. In particular, dense social networks, with high degrees of connectedness between people, such as in ethno-religious groups, close-knit neighbourhoods and the like, help establish norms of reasonableness about what is appropriate to feel, act and say. Karstedt (2002: 309) refers to these as 'fairness rules' and Nussbaum (2001) as 'norms of reasonableness', by which protagonists can determine what is prudent, sage and judicious, and conduct future relationships accordingly. In this sense, dense social networks represent 'communities of emotion' and the social relationships existing within them can, in part, make momentary emotions seem more permanent and reinforce the social practices they enact. People's social relations thus modulate their emotions, expurgating, intensifying or moderating them: in short, we become in our emotional repertoire like the people we associate closely with.

This view of emotions suggests, therefore, that compromise, when understood sociologically, does not require people after conflict to stop feeling or to suppress emotions; consensus needs to emerge around agreement to perform the ritualised behaviours and forms of talk that people may not personally feel, but which are recognised as socially productive for the restoration of moral sensibility in the future. This becomes feasible given people's participation in mutually reinforcing social networks where compromise is socially practised. Inasmuch as the social practice of compromise in public is now removed from private feelings, one of the key principles of the sociology of compromise is the distinction between public and private space, to which I now turn.

The public and private in sociology

Sociology has long theorised the character of public and private space (for a selection, see Bailey 2000; Kumar and Makarova 2008; Sennett (2003 [1974]), suggesting that the private sphere is the domestic sphere, the sphere of home – backstage to use Goffman's (1959) ubiquitous term – where people take off their overcoat, strip away the public mask and relax. The public is the sphere of social roles outside the home; the sphere of work, politics and civil society. In Goffman's dramaturgical terms it is frontstage space, not backstage, where we conform to public expecta-

THE SOCIOLOGY OF COMPROMISE AFTER CONFLICT   49

tions, act according to socially agreed roles and talk with a civil tongue (Kingwell 1995) and with the absence of 'hate speech' (Paris 2004: 184ff.).

Critically, however, this is not a simple distinction, for sociology no longer theorises it as a binary divide, for in late modernity the 'personalisation' and 'detraditionalisation' that characterises reflexive modernity has collapsed the distinction (Bailey 2000; on detraditionalisation, see Heelas, Lash and Morris 1995). The public and private penetrate each other – behaviour formerly restricted to the private sphere is now made into a public performance (politicians crying, open displays of grief, declarations of religious faith by public figures, and expressions of public anger and the like). For example, the personal has become political (Holmes 2000) and public space has been domesticated (Kumar and Makarova 2008: 332).

A sociology of compromise does not require the reinstatement of this as a binary divide. Compromise is the public performance of behaviours and language scripts that disguise private feelings and forms of talk, representing a 'surface' rather than 'deep' social practice, to use Hochschild's (2003) terms, one reproduced 'frontstage' with what Illouz (2007) calls 'cold intimacies', not with the full heartfelt passions of 'backstage'. This approach does not require that public and private spaces be hermetically sealed. After all, the performance of compromise in the public sphere is heavily influenced by private considerations and will oscillate according to the array of factors that prevent emotions momentarily being kept under management and control in public. Private factors – an anniversary, birthday, momentary reminders of the victim experience, flash memories provoked by music, television – penetrate the public performance of compromise.

There is another sense in which the public and private elide in compromise peace processes. Public space in these settings was rarely shared space. Public space mostly reflected the geography of the conflict, and either excluded minorities or involved a form of interaction that Goffman (1966) termed 'civil inattention', where people were aware of others but purposely practised inattention as a way of limiting direct interaction. With the peace process comes an increase in shared public spaces, in which people have to manage their own identity in relation to others in mixed settings in public; and to do so to a far greater extent than before (for Belfast, see Reid 2008).

These unauthentic performances of surface emotions in public are beneficial to peace. There are three conditions where compromise peace processes gain from non-authentic performances of surface emotions. The first condition is where the public good is served by the inauthentic performance of civility and tolerance in the public sphere, in language and behaviour. This condition holds true, of course, only when the compromise does not involve accommodation to human indignity and injustice, as Wolterstorff (2008) and Margalit (2010) would define it, and is reciprocal and fair. The second condition is when the compromise defends, protects and ensures people's moral rights. Moral rights are those entitlements people should expect by virtue of their moral character, where, to use the terminology of Peter Jones (2013), people are both *owed* certain sorts of conduct and where they are *wronged* if treated otherwise (see also Archard 2012; Jones 1994). In compromise peace processes, people are owed the moral right to be treated with civility and tolerance and are wronged when these are denied them. That is to say, compromise defends and protects people's moral rights after conflict. The third condition is when there are moral grounds for the public affirmation of the compromise, to the point where people are persuaded to be moral beacons despite private reservations. These moral grounds can involve the recognition that the collectivity benefits from the consensus against one's private interests, and that the compromise is reasonable in its outcomes for the collectivity as a whole, if not personally. These three conditions help establish sociologically why people might concur in public compromises that they may disagree with in private.

A sociology of compromise also requires us to explicate the social structural conditions which sustain or undermine these conditions. In my approach, compromise is envisaged as being easier for people to perform publicly according to several mediating factors, which I call 'compromise mediators'. Amongst them are included, for example, feelings of hope, the capacity for forgiveness, the ability to transcend divided memories of the former conflict, senses of the fairness of the concessions, views about whether in practice the concessions remain reciprocal, the social networks in which people are located, and social trust. We can briefly illustrate them.

Hope is interpersonal and sociological at the same time (on sociological treatments of hope, see Braithwaite 2004; Brewer 2010: 125–31). It describes the interpersonal process of anticipating some future desired state, but it is materially affected by the social conditions that help sustain the anticipating. The hoped-for goals can be individual or social, referring to personal aspirations for oneself or for society generally. Feelings of hope (that is, the capacity to anticipate) and the expectation of achieving goals in the future (personal and societal) will affect people's capacity to compromise. Hope and patience, however, should be run together, for it is worth distinguishing between patient and impatient hope – the willingness to wait or not for the anticipated goals. Late modernity suffers from instant gratification which undermines patience; this is even more so after conflict, when people want peace and want it now. Yet peace drops slow, as the Irish poet W.B. Yeats once penned, and sorely tests people's patience. Compromise requires the long view.

We are familiar with the suggestion that forgiveness has boundaries (Arendt 1958), even if the 'unforgivable' seems to be a very flexible category (Misztal 2011b), but memory and forgiveness are also normally understood as a couplet, because people's capacity to forgive is in common sense believed to be related to their ability to forget (hence the phrase 'to forgive and forget'). However, despite its advocacy as a post-conflict strategy for dealing with problematic memories (for example, Connerton 2008; Rieff 2016), forgetting can be impossible in the short to medium term. It is significant, therefore, that the sociology of compromise does not require forgetting in the private sphere, but a conscious decision in which people determine to transcend divided memories for the purposes of relational closeness in public space; the greater the capacity for transcendence, the more likelihood of garnering and sustaining compromise. People's sense of the fairness of the concessions, and that the concessions are reciprocal and are being kept to by all parties to them, also affect their capacity to compromise. That is, people's ability to fulfil their obligations is likely to diminish with the perception that the concessions are unequal or erstwhile opponents have abrogated their obligations. Reciprocity and fairness are therefore essential components of the sociology of compromise.

The social networks to which people belong and through which the management of emotions is partly accomplished also affects the social practice of compromise. The 'communities of emotion' that dense social networks constitute can support or undercut a person's capacity to compromise. Which of these outcomes transpires depends in some part on the quality of the social relations people had with protagonists prior to the conflict, and the impact that the violence had in restricting their post-conflict networks to their own group members. People's social connectedness with a like-minded social network of compromise is essential to its practice. Thus, both the level of social connectedness of people and the nature of those with whom they feel connected are important mediating considerations in the development of compromise.

This introduces the idea of social trust. The boundaries of compromise – like forgiveness – expand outwards with trust. Yet trust is the first casualty of communal conflict. Again, standard sociological ideas about trust can be used to support my approach to the sociology of compromise, for the dominant paradigm in sociology understands trust as related to the density of the social networks in which people participate (Lewis and Weigert 1985a, 1985b; Misztal 1996; Mollering 2001; Seligman 1997, 1998; Sztompka 1999). The more we interact with people known to each other, the greater our social capital, and the more willing we are to take the 'leaps of trust' (a phrase taken from Mollering 2001) in an otherwise untrustworthy world. Post-conflict societies are amongst the most untrusting, but trust can be garnered and practised where people participate in bridging social networks – networks of compromise if you will – where they learn that erstwhile enemies can be trusted. People with a 'victim identity' who are disconnected from social networks as a result of social withdrawal, or who restrict participation to partisan networks that do not bridge social divides, will remain untrusting or trustful of only their 'own' kind. This returns us to the earlier point. Compromise after conflict depends, in large part, on the quality of the social relations people had with protagonists prior to the conflict, and thus the impact that the violence had in restricting their post-conflict networks to members of their 'own' group.

These compromise mediators get to the kernel of sociology, for they show, using the terminology of C. Wright Mills' (1959b) characterisation of the sociological imagination, the intersection of people's personal biography, history, power, and the social structure. This is an interplay that represents sociology's unique promise, as Mills put it (for an application of Mills' ideas to a comparison of the peace processes in South Africa and Northern Ireland, see Brewer 2003). This interplay can be illustrated by research on the social practice of compromise in first-generation victims in Northern Ireland, South Africa and Sri Lanka (Brewer et al. 2017, 2018; Brewer, Hayes and Teeney 2018).

The capacity for forgiveness in first-generation victims in Sri Lanka, for example, was shaped by, amongst other things, the individual biography of faith commitment and the history of personal and family faith, as well as by the religious resources available culturally to victims to draw on in understanding the meaning and practice of forgiveness (Wijesinghe and Brewer 2018). Some Sri Lankan victims, for example, modelled their 'horizontal' forgiveness with others in personal relationships on the 'vertical' forgiveness they felt from their relationship with God. Forgiveness, however, is not dependent on personal faith, for secular forgiveness is real in some victims. Some victims explained their victimhood experience as leading to a loss or crisis of faith, making it critically important if forgiveness is to act as a compromise mediator, that there are alternative cultural resources to nurture its practice, such as cosmopolitan and humanitarian ethical systems. But forgiveness is also influenced by social structural conditions. Tamil victims in Sri Lanka, for example, were least forgiving and more revengeful than other Sri Lankan ethnic groups, because of the structural violence and disadvantage that is embedded in their double victimhood, where they experience not only their own conflict-related harm but also feelings of being vanquished and defeated as a group (on Tamil double victimhood, see Brewer et al. 2018: 165–78).

As another example of sociology's 'promise' with respect to understanding compromise, cross-communal social networks represent 'communities of compromise', but this mediator is arbitrated by all sorts of social structural, biographical and historical factors. These include victims' pre-conflict networks and friendship patterns, their biographical experiences of 'mixed' marriages and kinship patterns, the history of their encounters with 'the other' prior to the conflict, in terms of education, work, leisure and residential mixing, the nature of their victimhood experience and the background of those they blame for it, and so on. Cultural separateness can survive into compromise peace processes, and mixed social networks can be difficult to generate.

Cultural processes that affect the group have biographical meaning for individuals, encouraging some victims to experience group hurts as personal ones, and for group loyalties to supersede personal ones, which can result in some victims having strong senses of groups as victims. Group ties can affect how individual victims understand their biographical circumstances and emotionally process their victimhood, resulting in the development of a victim identity, frozen in the moment of their victimhood. This victim identity can have the consequence of social withdrawal or restricted social networks to people just like themselves, such as in their victim support group. This can facilitate bonding social capital, but not the bridging social capital that promotes communities of compromise (Graham 2018; see also Graham 2016; Leonard 2004). Social structure, history and biography elide in some first-generation victims to develop exclusive social networks that inhibit the social practice of compromise; others to inclusive social networks that constitute genuine communities of compromise.

One last example can suffice of the sociological imagination's promise with respect to understanding compromise mediators. The famous distinction made by Johan Galtung (1969) between negative and positive peace that dominates Peace Studies as an intellectual field, where negative peace is the ending of violence and positive peace the realisation of justice, fairness and equality of opportunity, and which I have reworked as a contrast between conflict transformation (negative peace) and social transformation (positive peace), bears directly on the significance of sociology's approach to compromise. Broader cultural and structural processes, such as poverty, inequality, social injustice, xenophobia and racism, can limit social transformation, resulting in limited social redistribution. Human rights may improve, but the material poverty of some victims can stay as bad as before, such that the violence associated with the conflict may have ended, but some victims are subject still to the structural violence of impoverishment and social injustice.

As one of the five antinomies discussed in Chapter 3, which represent the contrast between a broad and narrow notion of peace, the failure to undergo social transformation alongside conflict transformation potentially inhibits the social practice of compromise and makes it more challenging, negatively affecting compromise mediators. The lack of social transformation, for example, can undergird a view of the unfairness of the settlement, or support the view that others are not reciprocally sticking to their obligations under it, and persuade some first-generation victims to continue with distrust and unforgivingness, or to impose strict conditions on forgiveness, to lose hope in a better future, and to be unable to transcend the past and its divided memories. It can discourage an emotional empathy with the other that is the bedrock to the social practice of compromise, or, at best, make the social practice of compromise even more discomforting.

THE SOCIOLOGY OF COMPROMISE AFTER CONFLICT   55

In particular, social injustice destroys hope. The lower levels of hope amongst Tamils in Sri Lanka (Hayes and Brewer 2018), for example, point to the impact that structural disadvantage can have in denuding optimism and belief in progress in the future. There are some structural circumstances, however, where this does not happen. Where hope is delayed rather than denied, the aspiration to better times ahead is left open as a biographical experience, as is the case with many Black South Africans, who retain hopes for structural redistribution under Black majority rule in the future. For many of apartheid's victims, continued social injustice postpones rather than extinguishes hope. The risk for South Africa is that hope delayed turns eventually into hopelessness or anger.

This attention to first-generation victims' practice of compromise in the public sphere shows that first-generation victims have a level of magnanimity that turns them into moral beacons, with higher levels of moral sensibility, able to shine a light to the rest of society to follow (on victims as moral beacons, see Brewer and Hayes 2011b). This connects back to the way sociology understands peace discussed in Chapter 2, which is the restoration of social solidarity through a return to moral sensibility, and points to the major sociological contribution of the sociology of compromise.

The restoration of moral sensibility and solidarity with compromise

What is empirically interesting about this sociological conceptualisation of compromise is that most first-generation victims said they felt an impulse to *want* to get along with their erstwhile enemy, expressing a minimum moral consensus in which they say that their children and grandchildren must not go through what they have gone through.[1] This was expressed vividly by one Northern Irish victim: 'if the dead could speak, what would they say? Would they say – right be depressed, be angry, be an alcoholic, beat your wife, neglect your children? Or would they say, for [expletive deleted] sake, get up and get on with people.' Another victim put this forward focus on getting along in another way: 'the past does have important memories for people, but it doesn't count with the future plans for peace in lovingness and neighbourliness and getting on together. That is more important. People can think of the past if they so desire, but it doesn't come anywhere near tomorrow. Yesterday is over. Nothing can be done about it.' Such an approach to 'getting along'

56   ADVANCED INTRODUCTION TO THE SOCIOLOGY OF PEACE PROCESSES

was thought to be common amongst victims. As another remarked about fellow victims, 'my take on people is we're getting on'. 'Getting on' was their nomenclature for peace. As one said, 'there is no problem with me talking to them [former enemies] and getting on with them'.

Victims' personal preference for an ending to the violence and their hopes for a better future resulted, in most victims, in an interpersonal ethic, outworked in an ethical obligation to engage in social practices towards the other that support and undergird compromise. In the terms of Elias' figurational sociology, compromise is a civilising process that establishes civility in social relations, for this interpersonal ethic made compromise a moral virtue; something rooted in morality as much as political necessity, because the victimhood experience encodes what I refer to as a 'relational ethic' that makes most first-generation victims into moral beacons. In short, victimhood is a moral experience for most victims, with virtuous consequences. The paradox of this argument is that moral virtue emerges as the best outcome from the worst of experiences.

In some instances, this ethical obligation to 'getting along' was extended only to individual victims from the 'other' group or groups, but in some first-generation victims, it was extended to the group as a whole, affecting group relations not just interpersonal ones. This obligation to practise civility and tolerance existed despite the social stigma some victims can experience, or their disillusionment and disappointment with the progress of the social peace process. The majority of first-generation victims are surprisingly magnanimous, generous and empathetic towards their erstwhile enemies. Not all, nor for all of the time. As one victim remarked, 'the irony is that I now sit on committees with these very same people [former enemies]. And I get on famously. But I do most of the getting on. They do not have the same ability that I have as an individual.' Generosity can be more easily practised by those first-generation victims who have a survivor identity, eager to move on; least so by those with a victim's identity, fixed and frozen in the moment of their victimhood. As one respondent from Northern Ireland said of their victim identity, 'it is a blackness. To me it feels like a virus in my system that I cannot shake off. It is something every day I get up with. It is never far from my thoughts and it is never far from my feelings. It has destroyed my happiness. It has destroyed my family's happiness.' But even for others who are not locked into a victim identity, the interpenetration of public and private spaces can momentarily bring back bad memories and shift victims' emotional landscape temporarily, before it returns to the generosity, magnanimity and emotional empathy that represent its normal terrain.

Other studies of victims have referred to this magnanimity. In early work, Pumla Gobodo-Madikizela, a former member of the South African Truth and Reconciliation Commission, developed the idea of 'empathetic repair' (2008; see also 2012, 2016a, 2016b), which is the ethic of care many victims feel towards former perpetrators. The capacity for emotional empathy towards erstwhile enemies was the foundation of their renegotiation of the intersubjective relationship between them. As Gobodo-Madikizela (2016a: 13) argued, forgiveness is the wrong word for describing this emotional empathy. It extends beyond the willingness to forego what perpetrators might be thought to deserve; it is an ethic of care based on a deep understanding of the other's experience. This is the essence of the meaning of empathy (Gobodo-Madikizela 2016a: 13 defines empathy as the capacity to feel with, and to participate in, shared reflexive engagement with the other's inner life). In later work, she extends this argument further, referring to it as 'reparative humanism' (2020: 136–40), where emotional empathy with the erstwhile enemy extends to recognition of their humanity. In a telling passage she argues: 'the reciprocal mutuality of reparative humanism enables restoration of social bonds in a way that opens up new relational possibilities in the aftermath of violence' (Gobodo-Madikizela 2020: 140). Others have used the notion of reparative humanism in different contexts and grounding it in different moral frameworks. Paul Gilroy (2017), for example, applies Frantz Fanon's humanism that raged against the structural inequality and injustice in Global North–South relations, to establish an anti-colonial, non-racial re-enchantment of human dignity.

The suggestion that victims seek to restore social bonds, despite their victimhood, is the key to my argument about social compromise and moral sensibility, although I assert it to be *because* of their victimhood, not despite it. Such a view, however, challenges what I call the Holocaust model of victimhood, especially the well-cited arguments of Hannah Arendt (1958) that acts of 'radical evil' are neither punishable nor forgivable. Emotional empathy and reparative humanism towards former enemies also runs counter to the rather pejorative attention victims normally receive in peace processes, where the emphasis is on what Mihai (2016) calls their negative emotions. This is because legacy issues are located overwhelmingly in terms of the new field of transitional justice studies, with its emphasis on negative emotions through reintegrative shaming (on which, see Brewer 2010: 119–25). In transitional justice, the debate appropriates the Holocaust model in which victims' emotional repertoire becomes one about trauma, shame, guilt, anger and retribution. This overlooks first-generation victims' future-focused emotions, as I call them, which makes them moral beacons. (These concerns are the subject of Chapter 5, so further discussion at this juncture is delayed.)

Suffice to say here, it is important to note that moral sensibility is the *outcome* of compromise not its cause; compromise creates the conditions for the restoration of moral sensibility and social solidarity, not the other way round. This capacity to be moral beacons because of their high levels of moral sensibility is embedded in the social practice of compromise. The wish to 'get along' with their erstwhile enemy that most first-generation victims exemplify, the hope that their children and grandchildren will have a better future and never have their victimhood experience, ethically obligates most victims towards the public practice of moral sensibility, civility and tolerance, regardless of how discomforting this is or what they feel, say and do in private. There might still be fear and anxiety rooted in their victimhood, but feelings of obligation to the next generation mean they try to rise above it. 'Getting along' after conflict becomes a minimum moral standard, an intersubjective 'relational' ethic if you like, that is the direct opposite to what moral philosophers call a 'subjective ethic', where the moral duty is to oneself alone. 'Getting along' becomes an intersubjective ethic, where the moral duty is to improving relationships with others for the sake of the future. It is worth quoting one Northern Irish victim's account of the obligation they felt under to help other victims less able to 'get along' with erstwhile enemies. 'I enjoy helping other people, who have not actually got to the stage where I am at. Who are still suffering. And there is still people who are really suffering badly with Post Traumatic Stress Disorder and all that, and can't get over it. And there is people that feel the hatred that you were speaking about. I feel that I can get through to those people and help them as best I can.' Another said: 'I think nowadays everything is moving to the centre and people are getting on better and mixing better. And I think [this helps] people to realise what other people and other communities have suffered.' In short, this relational ethic also undergirds the help some first-generation victims give to others to assist them to better 'get along', by facilitating in other victims the practice of compromise.

The implications of this argument are very profound. The social practice of compromise allows the reproduction of society itself through the restoration of moral sensibility, making it possible for people to live together in social solidarity after conflict. Compromise, in short, facilitates the social practice of sociability after conflict. This is a situational ethic grounded in people's capacities to want people to get along, and to want society to work after conflict. It is a situational ethic because while this relational ethic may be shaped by some over-arching ethical system, so many victims said they were non-religious, had a crisis of faith because of their victimhood, or grounded their practice of forgiveness, as one of its outworkings, in secular belief systems. Hence, I argue that this relational ethic is encoded in the situatedness of the victimhood experience itself. This relational ethic is outworked in the majority of first-generation victims in an enhanced emotional empathy with other victims across the communal divide, and in an ethical obligation to 'get along', which leads to all the forms of talk and performances described above, that mark the social practices through which moral sensibility is restored.

An interesting sociological question follows from this argument. What are the critical differences that explain why some second- and third-generation victims have less moral sensibility than their parents and grandparents, and are more angry, intolerant, and uncompromising? This highlights some of the social structural problems involved in the restoration of moral sensibility and social solidarity after conflict. If it is the victimhood experience itself that obligates 'getting along', subsequent generations by definition lack the direct experience of victimhood in which 'getting along' is situationally located.

Second-generation victims of apartheid in particular are very angry, rooted in the structural failure of the post-apartheid state to deliver socio-economic redistribution and social justice (Mueller-Hirth 2018). Some young South Africans are very angry at their parents for being too morally sensible, too tolerant and forgiving of apartheid's beneficiaries. First-generation Tamil victims also warned of the risk in Sri Lanka if poverty, disadvantage and unemployment were not eliminated. Even the 'peace generation' of young people in Northern Ireland, more economically privileged than in the other two societies, refer to some disillusionment and disappointment (Smith 2018). The sociability generated by this relational ethic in most first-generation victims need not necessarily restore humane co-existence, if subsequent generations fail to gain the

60   ADVANCED INTRODUCTION TO THE SOCIOLOGY OF PEACE PROCESSES

peace dividend in terms of structural and material improvement in their lives. Inter-generational victimhood thus impacts on this relational ethic to weaken its reproduction of moral sensibility and social solidarity when, as I said in Chapter 2, social transformation does not accompany conflict transformation.

This suggests that the relational ethic is temporal. It is temporal in two senses. First, it can be undercut over time, even for first-generation victims where they continue to experience structural violence and disadvantage, so that poverty and impoverishment undermine the wish to 'get along', and thus the situated motivation to moral sensibility that lies within this relational ethic. It is also temporal in another sense, for second and third generations, lacking the direct victimhood experience of the past generations, can have higher levels of unforgivingness and anger than their parents and grandparents, because moral sensibility is not situated in the ethic to 'get along'.

Conclusion

The social peace process involves people learning to live together after conflict; it is about healing in society. This means the restoration of broken relationships and the development of trust and respect between people and communities. The political peace process is not irrelevant to this, but a focus on the institutional reform of governance structures through statebuilding can divert attention away from peacebuilding in the social peace process. Efficiency in the *means* of governance after conflict, important as this is, should never replace the improvement in the lives of ordinary men and women as the primary *goal* of the social peace process. This is the opportunity for sociology to intervene in the analysis of peace and compromise peace processes.

A sociological approach to compromise, as one such intervention, has shown that, while all victims of conflict struggle with the past, the majority do not want to remain living in it. They all live with the past, but the majority do not want to live in the past. As a Northern Irish victim put it, 'if you get the balance wrong, if you are living in the past too much you are stuck in that'. The social practice of compromise, and through it the restoration of moral sensibility, is not easy, but most victims have a 'relational ethic', as I call it, that makes them moral beacons. Victims are ethical beings; and most have an intersubjective, relational ethic that reflects in seeking meaningful relationships with others which prioritises 'getting along'. This relational ethic is situational in that it is grounded in the victimhood experience itself rather than a single over-arching ethical framework like religion or secular humanism. I argue that this relational ethic is encoded in the situatedness of the victimhood experience itself. The victimhood experience persuades most victims that they have to commit to change in order to 'get along' with others and for this to 'never happen again'. This relational ethic is outworked in the majority of victims in an enhanced emotional empathy with other victims across the communal divide in order to 'get along'. As one Northern Irish victim said of other victims, 'they are getting along because they have to get along'. And this relational ethic is premised on all the forms of talk and actions by which compromise is socially practised and from which moral sensibility is reproduced.

The social practice of compromise makes moral sensibility, civility and tolerance possible, but it works, as we have emphasised, under the constraints and opportunities of social structure, personal biography and history, and its potential is affected by compromise mediators that press heavily upon it. The ethical obligation can quickly disappear if structural reform is missing, especially for second- and third-generation victims. Second and third generations of victims lack this relational ethic and can show a level of unforgivingness and anger that is at odds with the emotional empathy of their parents and grandparents, meaning that they lose the ethical obligation to want to 'get along'. Social transformation is not only important to bolster the relational ethic of first-generation victims; it addresses the anger of their children and grandchildren at the continuance of social injustice, which can be experienced as a form of social pain. As one respondent said, 'there is pain. A lot of pain in this society.'

This interrogation of compromise has highlighted the importance of the emotional landscape of people in compromise peace processes, and of the emotional interiority of people learning to live together in moral sensibility after conflict. The sociology of compromise opens up discussion of an array of cognitive issues vital to the restoration of moral sensibility and social solidarity, and thus to the success of compromise peace processes. These cognitive issues include anger, forgiveness, mercy, forgetting, hope, trust and memory, amongst others. The Holocaust model of victimhood thus is inappropriate to many modern conflicts. These concerns are taken up in the next chapter. The distinction transitional justice studies makes between positive and negative emotions, in order to understand the impact of these emotions on peace processes, is not helpful; far better to contrast past-focused and future-focused emotions.

NOTE

1. All the following quotations are taken from the Leverhulme study of victims in Northern Ireland, South Africa and Sri Lanka; see Brewer, Hayes and Teeney 2018; Brewer et al. 2018.

5 The sociology of post-conflict emotions

Introduction

The return of emotions in sociology is part of the second cognitivist revolution in sociology and social science generally, which reflects the re-enchantment of sociology's focus and discourse around concern with affective and moral issues like love, hate, suffering, mercy, forgiveness, hope, anger, human dignity and the like. The political economy of re-enchantment, discussed in Chapter 2, locates these affective and moral concerns in material and structural conditions within late modernity. The emergence of a sociology of peace processes fits within this context and is part of this political economy; the sociology of peace processes, in turn, is centrally concerned with these cognitive issues and their relevance to peacebuilding.

The emotional landscape of people in societies emerging out of conflict has mostly been understood through what I call the Holocaust model of victimhood. This model sets up a simple binary between apolitical, powerless and innocent victims, killed solely for their identity, versus evil perpetrators who murder groundlessly. This overlooks the problem of multiple victimhood, where people belong to groups that are simultaneously victims and perpetrators (Brewer 2010: 123ff.), and the moral claims to virtuous violence by perpetrators (Brewer 2021a). More pertinent to the argument here, this model isolates the focus on to emotions like revenge, shame, guilt, resentment and retribution, based on Arendt's view that there are limits to forgiveness after mass atrocities like the Holocaust. Inasmuch as they principally address the legacy of conflict, transitional justice studies discuss emotions extensively, but couch the debate within the Holocaust model by its narrow emphasis on guilt and reintegrative shaming (Braithwaite 2020; Braithwaite and Mugford 1994; Scheff 2000, 2011a). This explains why Karstedt (2002) describes the return of emotions in transitional justice studies as the return of shame, why Brudholm (2008) sees resentment as virtuous, and why attention is given to what the field calls 'negative emotions' (Mihai 2016).

This chapter takes the opposite approach, using a sociological lens to critique the distinction between negative and positive emotions by offering an alternative formulation of past-focused and future-focused emotions. This allows us to rethink the connection between emotions and peacebuilding in the social peace process. Emergent sociologies of shame, rage and revenge (for example Ray, Smith and Wastell 2004; Scheff 1994, 2000, 2011a, 2011b) and retribution (Elster 2004: 129ff.) are thus inadequate representations of people's emotional landscape after conflict. The moral sensibilities embedded in the victimhood experience discussed in Chapter 4, with the emphasis on empathetic repair and reparative humanism (Gobodo-Madikizela 2016a, 2016b, 2020), is the foundation to this chapter's outline of the emergent sociologies of anger, forgiveness, mercy, social trust and hope.

A critique of emotions in transitional justice studies

The burgeoning field of the sociology of emotions has yet to be applied to understand the range of emotions involved in peace processes, and emotions are still in the shadowlands within transitional justice studies, where they are mentioned largely in routine ways, mostly in terms of the legacy of violence, with a limited range of emotions in view. Emotions like anger, hatred and revenge get raised in discussions of victims; shame–guilt in respect of restorative justice approaches to ex-combatants; and fear, anxiety and distrust in relation to the problems of dealing with the past. This isolates specific emotions and tends to direct attention onto what are called 'negative emotions'. A similar emphasis is not placed on the corollary of 'positive emotions', such as hope, forgiveness, compassion, empathy, tolerance, mercy and humanitarian sensibility. While forgiveness has been widely canvassed as one positive emotion in the transitional justice literature, it is strongly associated with Christian eschatology, which makes it problematic in the secularised West and to the majority in the non-Christian Global South.

Emotions like guilt, anger and forgiveness are more subtle in their effects on peacebuilding than the distinction between negative and positive emotions suggests. The need for more subtle approaches to emotions after conflict can be illustrated with respect to guilt. Shame–guilt reintegration is too limiting a lens through which to understand guilt. When we sociologically deconstruct guilt, we see that peacebuilding provokes five particular forms of guilt that require distinction. Each deserves more attention in the study of peace processes. I call them

- bystander guilt (the guilt feelings amongst those who stood by and did nothing actively for peace);
- survivor guilt (feelings of guilt amongst victims for not having been killed in incidents that took others and which tends to lead to enhanced emotional empathy with other survivors);
- perpetrator guilt (the feelings of remorse amongst those who participated in the violence);
- cultural guilt (guilt feelings that shape cultural responses to past violence and help towards mobilising senses of cultural trauma); and
- guilt denial (forms of justification and normalisation that declare there is nothing to be remorseful for, the very expression of which often leads to emotional responses and reactions from others).

The sociologist Jon Elster's (2004) approach to the problem of transitioning societies focused on the first and third types, the discipline of transitional justice studies focuses primarily on the third type, trauma and psychotherapy studies the second, cultural sociologists on the fourth (Alexander 2012), while criminological studies of ex-combatants make us fully aware of the fifth. While all five forms of guilt are important to understanding the legacy problem of dealing with the past, which is the problematic that drives transitional justice studies as a discipline, I suggest, however, that bystander guilt is particularly relevant. It evokes Freud's idea of repression, in which the bystander projects their guilt at doing nothing on to perpetrators, who thereby become scapegoated (see Moses 2021 for a discussion of scapegoating and victimhood). Bystander guilt allows us to compare the way in which bystanders can thus have higher levels of unforgivingness and retribution compared to many victims (see, in particular, Elster 2004). For example, survey data from the Northern Ireland Leverhulme study, that compared victims and non-victims, shows victims to have higher levels of moral sensibility (Brewer and Hayes 2011b), to be more positive in their opinion towards the Good Friday Agreement (Brewer and Hayes 2013), to be more forgiving towards ex-prisoners (Brewer and Hayes 2015a) and more positive in their response to a range of legacy policies for dealing with the past (Brewer and Hayes 2015b). While not all non-victims are bystanders in the sense used here, some were, but the survey material successfully demonstrates the empathetic response that victimhood garners, and which bystanders and others lack.

Guilt, in other words, is a more complex emotion than the attention on perpetrators' guilt that dominates the reintegrative shaming approach of transitional justice studies. This feeds into my view that there are two special problems with the treatment of emotions in transitional justice studies, which give me two points of departure for the next stages of this chapter.

First, there are distinct stages in peacebuilding, and emotions emerge as an issue quite differently in each, with specific emotions assuming importance at different stages. Second, the range of emotions displayed within the Holocaust model of reintegrative shaming are very narrow, and the emotional landscape in societies emerging out of conflict needs to be reconceptualised to configure a broader array of emotions. The sociological imagination proves fruitful when doing this.

Coming to my first point of departure, there are three stages to a process of peacebuilding, and emotions impact on them quite differently. There are

- the emotions aroused during the conflict by the violence itself, emotions which are left as a legacy of the violence and which need to be managed in the peace negotiation phase, such as mistrust, hate, grief and loss;
- the emotions aroused by the idea of peace itself and the emotional adjustments which either non-violence or dramatically reduced levels of violence provoke during the post-conflict phase, such a rethinking our conceptions of the 'other' and of who the enemy now is; and
- the emotions invoked by having to learn to live together in tolerance once the conflict is over, either for the first time or after a long time, such as past-focused emotions like fear, guilt, anger and shame,

and future-focused emotions like compassion, forgiveness, emotional empathy and restorative humanism.

For example, fear, mistrust, anger, guilt, revenge, hate, compassion, hope and empathy are all part of the emotional landscape that protagonists bring with them to the table when discussing a second preference peace settlement; and some cause negotiators problems in trying to convince the protagonists to stay at the table. Not many political scientists would accept this but managing the emotional dynamics of peace discussions is as important as the political deals they discuss. Another of the realities overlooked in transitional justice studies is that peace itself comes with an emotional cost (Brewer 2010: 36). I mean more than the suffering people endured so that others can experience the benefits of peace – the grief, depression, suicidal feelings, and feelings of loss and pain that victims and survivors live with daily. People have to recalibrate who the enemy is and thus reassess their own identity in relation to those who, perhaps for a very long time, have been considered outsiders (Lederach 1997 refers to this as the identity dilemma). Peace itself can cause a whole range of emotions – fear, anxiety, suspicion, mistrust – in response to this ontological readjustment.

One thing should be clear by now: the same narrow range of emotions recur in discussions of emotions in transitional justice studies. I suggest this is because the different stages a peace process goes through isolate past-focused emotions in ways that reinforce their prominence in public debate. Debate about the legacy of the conflict will always emerge in the post-conflict phase, giving the past an unwarranted role as the arbiter of the future. Discussions about the past are backward looking, so that emotions that might direct society's attention to the future – what I call future-focused emotions – are made secondary to those emotions provoked by discussions of the morality of the past. Fear, mistrust, revenge, anger and hate become the currency, and those groups most likely to feel, express and perform these emotions are the stakeholders who are given public attention. It is for this reason that debates about emotions in transitional justice almost exclusively focus only on victims and perpetrators.

Towards a sociology of post-conflict emotions

Deeply profound questions need to be asked about the emotional landscape of societies emerging out of conflict. What are the emotional inhibitors and the emotional enablers that affect peace? I ask that question knowing fully that it is not a question that is even posed in transitional justice studies, let alone one that has answers. This is yet more reason why emotions need to emerge from the shadows in the study of peace processes. I suggest the sociology of peace processes offers fruitful advances.

This brings me to my second point of departure. In order to illustrate the need for a new conceptual map through which we might better understand the problem of emotions in societies emerging out of conflict, I want to isolate five emotions – anger, hope, forgiveness, mercy and social trust – to show their subtlety and complexity. By using a sociological approach to reconceptualise them, we can illuminate the inadequacy of current mapping and better highlight their future-focused role in peacebuilding. I am aware that emotions are always closely linked, but I want to isolate them for purposes of conceptual mapping.

A sociology of anger

It is often said by peacebuilders that people should not get angry, they should get change instead. This negative view of anger is naïve. We need to better understand anger as an emotion and its important contribution to peacebuilding as a future-focused emotion. Peace processes often provide no appropriate cultural space for expressions of people's anger, grief, loss, pain and suffering. The moral obligation placed upon victims to 'forgive', to 'move on', to 'put the past behind them', and to 'forget', means these cultural spaces are few, especially in the public sphere. This is because 'anger' is thought of as dysfunctional to peace. However, to see anger as dysfunctional is to view it too narrowly.

I suggest we need to distinguish three types of anger in peacebuilding:

- righteous anger (justified and merited, but expressed and enacted within fairness rules that are orientated in its effects to others);
- self-righteous anger (justified and merited, but expressed and enacted without fairness rules, so that it is self-oriented rather than oriented to the other); and

THE SOCIOLOGY OF POST-CONFLICT EMOTIONS   69

- unrighteous anger (unjustified and unmerited but expressed and enacted regardless).

Use of the term righteousness as the structuring variable in the typology of anger needs to be explained. Righteousness appears over five hundred times in the Talmud and more than two hundred times in the New Testament. It is mentioned several times in the Quran. Most of these references, however, refer to the injunction to be religiously righteous, the quality of holiness, purity and piousness as laid out in these particular scriptures. The emphasis on righteousness in this typology is not intended to evoke the long tradition in all the world religions that address its doctrinal features, but to link back to the emphasis on moral sensibility as the cornerstone of the sociological approach to peace. This is not the same as holiness and piety. Righteousness literally means to be right; specifically, to be morally right and justified.

Righteous anger reflects this in two ways: the anger is legitimate, or to use Brudholm's (2008) term it has virtue, because of the victimhood and suffering that was experienced; and the anger is conducted morally within fairness rules that do not morally enervate the opponent. Righteous anger does the 'right thing' for *other* people rather than oneself. Self-righteous anger is morally right only in the first sense, in that it is morally justifiable given the victimhood, but it is self-centred, focused on the moral enervation of the other; it is not morally right in the second sense. Unrighteous anger has no claim to moral rightness in either sense. It can be faux anger, an anger that should not bear its name because it is manufactured and manipulated; it is not morally merited and is unjustified. Not all anger is therefore virtuous or legitimate.

A lot of the anger that pours out on the streets by crowds of people during the travails of a peace process, and which is thought to be dysfunctional to people learning to live together, is self-righteous or unrighteous anger. These are forms of anger, whether merited or not in terms of levels of suffering, which are not empathetic towards the other. They are made out of rage, perhaps even revenge, and seek to strip the other of human dignity and respect. Righteous anger, on the other hand, is functional in peace processes; it allows people's narratives to be heard rather than repressed; it overcomes silent, voiceless suffering, and when accompanied with a fairness rule that ensures the 'other' is not morally enervated and stripped of human dignity, it can restore broken relationships at the same time. It

70   ADVANCED INTRODUCTION TO THE SOCIOLOGY OF PEACE PROCESSES

follows, therefore, that social spaces need to be created for the expression
of righteous anger, which I refer to as 'listening spaces' (Brewer 2018b) in
which people can hear the narratives of each other.

It is through this empathetic sharing that righteous anger can enhance
mutual understanding, build trust, erode negative stereotypes, and facilitate inclusive and mixed social networks, the very compromise mediators
that promote the social practice of moral sensibility, civility and tolerance.
Righteous anger in victims can thus enhance emotional empathy, not
destroy it, and when this type of anger works alongside the social practice
of compromise, it can permit the possibility for first-generation victims
to be moral beacons to the rest of society (Brewer 2018b: 244–5). It is
self-righteous and unrighteous anger that makes anger a problem in peace
processes.

A sociology of forgiveness

Inasmuch as the moral obligation to forgive squeezes the cultural space
for the expression and enactment of righteous anger and reduces the
number of 'listening spaces' where each other's righteous anger can be
heard, forgiveness is not the panacea it is claimed to be in peace processes,
for it too can be dysfunctional. Forgiveness is also simultaneously more
subtle and complicated than the current literature accepts.

Forgiveness can be defined as intentional forbearance of the emotional
and behavioural reactions that harm would otherwise deserve in order
to continue with or restore social relationships (Brewer 2018b: 246).
This does not involve the offending action being sanitised, normalised or
made excusable; and the responses it provokes in those who are harmed
are not denied, undervalued or diminished. Forgiveness means pardon-
ing the action *despite* its wrongfulness and refusing to respond to it in
ways that might otherwise be expected or deserved. Forgiveness does
not suggest that perpetrators deserve to be forgiven; nor should victims
lose sight of perpetrators' culpability and deem themselves so lacking in
esteem and moral worth as not to protest their victimhood. Forgiveness
needs to be understood in a way that makes clear that perpetrators forego
what is otherwise deserved, and that no denial or denuding of the moral
wrongfulness of the acts is implied by forgiving them. Sociology helps in
deconstructing what this involves.

THE SOCIOLOGY OF POST-CONFLICT EMOTIONS   71

A sociology of forgiveness distinguishes between three kinds of forgiveness (these ideas have been expanded further in Brewer 2010: 131–9; Brewer 2018b: 246–9):

- Two-party forgiveness. This is the conventional kind, modelled on religious forms. It is exogenous, coming from the outside, whether from God, the injured faction or both. This grants the power to forgive to the other party, equating forgiveness with the issuing of the pardon and the mercifulness shown in not responding in ways that otherwise would be justified, leaving the first party powerless, dependent on the other's magnanimity.
- One-party forgiveness. This is self-forgiving, and it is endogenous, coming from within, which is what forgiving oneself literally means. We have the capacity to forgive ourselves, separate from another's forgiveness of us, and can engage in repair independent of it by carrying our forgiveness of ourselves into forgiving those whom we need to.
- Third-party forgiveness. This involves people forgiving on others' behalf for wrongs done to the collectivity in figurative and symbolic ways. Other parties for whom the conflict was experienced as personal can become forgivers with respect to their *own* individual responsibilities, as a result of the figurative and symbolic acts of forgiveness displayed by third parties.

These are not hierarchical. The first type, the classic two-party forgiveness, for example, is often the least efficacious. Its ubiquity indeed is in part because it is the most unforgiving type (Brewer 2018b: 248). It is the most challenging form of forgiveness because it imposes on perpetrators obligations to specific formulations of wording, specific acts of contrition and public expressions of remorse that are almost impossible to make. It is also the most religiously conservative form of forgiveness, allowing people to draw on religious themes and precepts as reasons *not* to forgive, because the request for forgiveness does not conform in word or deed to religious ideas of forgiveness in Judeo-Christian scripture.

Given that two-party forgiveness is prosaically understood as the only kind in which victim and perpetrator come together to initiate the exchange of apology, pardon and redemption, third-party forgiveness might be thought of as no forgiveness at all. On the contrary, it can be very effective as an alternative to two-party forgiveness. The redemptive value of forgiveness is more likely to be realised when forgiveness is done in symbolic form, precisely because it is not dependent on the other party

72   ADVANCED INTRODUCTION TO THE SOCIOLOGY OF PEACE PROCESSES

fulfilling their part face-to-face. When co-presence reignites emotional feelings, making it harder to ask for or grant forgiveness, one or both parties can rile against the others' refusal to the point where the exchange degenerates into mutual recriminations, with no knock-on effect for the quality of other relationships. For these reasons, figurative rather than literal forgiveness is always likely to be more redemptive.

Forgiveness in figurative form is done via public statements in the press, on television, at 'truth' recovery forums, such as public enquiries and 'truth' commissions, in civil society workshops, seminars or public lectures devoted to the topic, at citizenship education forums, during religious services, debates in parliament and political assemblies, or in submissions at courts of law. Figurative forgiveness can be expressed and enacted also in everyday life. Various interaction rituals (Brewer 2010: 137) can be performed that speak to people's figurative forgiveness of others to whom they have no personal obligation, such as street marches, art and photographic exhibitions, new forms of memory work by women's groups, schools and civil society groups, and rituals of empathetic repair between neighbours, in supermarkets, church pews and on sports fields. These settings constitute what we might call 'social spaces of forgiveness–redemption'. Some of these spaces and rituals are clearly religious, where public theologies of forgiveness are performed in prayer (Torrance 2006), expressed also in hymnody and song, as well as public statements by Church leaders, but secular spaces are also readily adaptable for rituals of forgiveness and redemption.

It is the *publicness* of the emotional display in figurative forgiveness that brings greatest redemptive value, for even if we can imagine a situation in which the injured party would prefer the request to be made face-to-face in order to agree to forgive, this repairs only the interpersonal relationship. The redemption earned by public statements, however, is experienced vicariously by many of the witnesses to them, for whom the statements speak to their own circumstances. This socially disseminates the effect of the public statements broadly to a 'community of forgivers' that has been touched by the public statements. Third-party forgiveness can create a public climate in which a thousand acts of private repentance become possible, as people forgive others interpersonally as a result of experiencing generous acts of third-party forgiveness. Such figurative forgiveness gives meaning to Prager's (2008: 416–17) idea of 'redres-

THE SOCIOLOGY OF POST-CONFLICT EMOTIONS   73

sive communities', which become 'communities of forgiveness' (Brewer 2018b: 248).

A sociology of mercy

There has been too much focus on forgiveness in the literature and not enough on mercy. Part of the problem with forgiveness is its conditionality. It can be difficult for forgiveness to be practised when strict conditions are wrapped around it that almost encourage unforgivingness. These conditions arise with the Judeo-Christian view that forgiveness has to be deserved; to forego punishment, people must first show they deserve pardon. This is an unhelpful power asymmetry. It is for this reason that perhaps the better emotion in these transitional settings is mercy.

Mercy is not a concept discussed in the literature on legacy issues because of its religious connotations and its link to Christian eschatology. In its religious sense it refers to notions like charity, grace and leniency in forbearing punishment when it is deserved. A putative sociology of mercy would denude it of such overtones and identify its secular manifestations. A sociology of mercy might define mercy along the following lines: mercy is the practice of compassion and clemency towards someone whom we have the power to punish, requiring from them no response in return and without conditions attached. On the basis of this definition, a sociology of mercy would, I suggest, include five constituent elements: (a) *the social practices of mercy*, the rituals, behaviours and interactions through which mercy is constituted, such as by forgiveness, social trust, practising the politics of grace, courtesy and good will, by clemency, emotional empathy and reparative humanism; (b) *the social spaces for mercy*, the physical and social spaces in which we can practise mercy, such as 'listening spaces', 'social spaces of forgiveness–redemption', new forms of memory work in civil society where we transcend divisive social memories, and spaces where, to use another term of mine, we remember forwards to the future (Brewer 2020); (c) *the historical geography of mercy*, the areas, regions and historical cases where mercy has been practised, and which can be located in the context of the people who practised it and the social factors that explain their practice; (d) *the materiality of mercy*, meaning the attention to issues of social injustice, inequality and colonial dispossession that provoke the need for mercy and explain its practice; and (e) *the limits of mercy*, which refers to the structural constraints that limit mercifulness,

74 ADVANCED INTRODUCTION TO THE SOCIOLOGY OF PEACE PROCESSES

the categories of people and groups, and the forms of harm that make mercifulness difficult.

Mercy needs to be mapped sociologically in these sorts of ways, so that its application and practice in transitional societies can compensate for the deficiencies in the notion and practice of forgiveness. Regretfully, however, forgiveness and forgetting (see Rieff 2016) are the terms of debate. Sociologists of mercy might enter this debate and challenge the terms on which it is currently conducted.

A sociology of social trust

Mercy implicates the idea of social trust. One of the social practices of mercy is trust; trust that the wrongdoer, who evades punishment and who has nothing required of them to be treated mercifully, will not offend and harm again. Trust is thus critical to the practice of mercy.

It is necessary to consider two types of trust as they connect to peace processes – political and social trust. In conflict transformation, political trust works between warring political groups enough to bring them to the negotiation table, stay there, and to commit to a political settlement. In social transformation, social trust works between ordinary men and women to facilitate healing, reconciliation and tolerance in society. Political trust is thus part of the process of conflict transformation in the political peace process, and social trust part of the process of social transformation in the social peace process.

We no longer believe that social trust is based on economic self-interest, as Utilitarianism in the nineteenth century once argued, but rather, as the sociologist Anthony Giddens (1990) puts it, trust is based on the capacity for confidence in the reliability of people, institutions and structures. This embeds social trust in the quality of social relationships rather than on calculations of self-interest. However, violence destroys sociability, and societies emerging out of conflict are thereby marked by the absence of social trust. Rebuilding it is one of the goals of the social peace process.

Social trust is grounded in the quality and frequency of our personal relationships. Sociologists see it as rooted in the density of the social networks in which people are located (for example Misztal 1996; Sztompka 2008). The more people in social networks know each other, the more friends

THE SOCIOLOGY OF POST-CONFLICT EMOTIONS   75

and acquaintances are themselves linked, the denser social networks become, from which develops what Sztompka (2008) calls 'trust cultures'. Social trust is like kindness or respect; it spreads around amongst people linked in bonds of friendship, expanding with the boundaries of social interaction.

Late modern society, however, is becoming less and less capable of social trust. Sociologists refer to late modern society as the risk society (Beck 1992, 1999), with traditional structures linked to religion, close-knit neighbourhoods and dense social networks losing their ability to shape social life, which both increases vulnerabilities and increases sensitivity to, and awareness of, these vulnerabilities. The boundaries of social trust have narrowed as a result of profound social changes. Close-knit community structures have been replaced by more mobile and frenetic forms of social life that transcend local space and time. Social networks that defined the trustworthiness of people, institutions and structures have become disembedded from local family and community structures, and from neighbourhood-based friendship patterns. Senses of place are now global rather than local. Thus, we now have long-distance families, with their sense of themselves as a family unit kept alive by extended social processes and technology. Social relationships and friendships are no longer embedded in personal relations in local place and space, so that social trust is no longer spatial and localised. Social trust therefore needs to be reproduced over extended distances, often by forms of social media and telecommunication that have replaced the face-to-face personal relations that formerly grounded social trust and defined the people who were considered trustworthy. One of the significant social changes that has occurred as modernity has advanced is that we have moved from social trust to social untrustworthiness as the default social condition.

One of the acute ways that ordinary people have experienced the profound social changes in family and community structures, and in the faster pace of social life that have occurred in their lifetime, is through the narrowing of the boundaries of social trust. Place alone no longer confers confidence in the reliability of people, institutions and community structures. Social trust is no longer a natural part of the social and cultural obligations that formed the local community to which they belonged; they now have to learn, sometimes through bitter experience, who they can trust in a risky and vulnerable society. It is for this reason that Mollering (2001) refers to people in modern societies having to learn the confidence to take 'leaps

76 ADVANCED INTRODUCTION TO THE SOCIOLOGY OF PEACE PROCESSES

of trust' in face of the threatening 'unknowables' that shape their expectations of trustworthiness.

This significant social change exacerbates the problem of social trust in transitioning societies, as people learn to live together in tolerance after conflict. Conflict polarises people and severely contracts and narrows the boundaries of the people considered as trustworthy. Post-conflict societies are therefore amongst the most untrusting. This imposes a significant burden on peace processes, and the extent to which social trust has been garnered offers a measure against which we can gauge the success of negotiated second preference peace settlements.

To understand the scale of the problem in restoring social trust after conflict, I wish to make two sets of distinctions. We might call the first distinction between 'surface' and 'deep' social trust, and the second between 'particularised' compared to 'generalised' social trust. The distinction between 'surface' and deep' social trust describes the level of trust; the distinction between 'particularised' and 'generalised' social trust describes the stages through which we broaden who it is that is considered trustworthy.

Let me come first to the issue of who is considered trustworthy. In the study of victims in Northern Ireland, South Africa and Sri Lanka (Brewer, Hayes and Teeney 2018; Brewer et al. 2018) only a very small minority of victims reported a complete lack of social trust in the former enemy, such as this victim when referring to Catholics. 'You couldn't trust them, no way could you trust them. You could be chatting to them in the morning and then they could be behind a ditch and shoot you the next day. How would you come to a compromise with those people?' Instead, most first-generation victims were prepared to take 'the leap of trust'. The majority of these did so, however, in a two-stage process. The key here is to slowly extend outwards the boundaries of those who can be trusted, to cover individual members of the erstwhile enemy groups rather than the collectivity as a whole. That is, social trust is first possible in a particularised way, extended to individuals known or who become known, as part of the victims' social network, making them able to trust individuals from the other community whom they knew and encountered, but not yet the 'other' group as a whole. It is trust on a one-to-one basis as the situation demands it. From this, particularised social trust can then, hopefully,

THE SOCIOLOGY OF POST-CONFLICT EMOTIONS   77

follow generalised social trust, in which negative stereotypes and myths about the whole group are replaced by social trust.

With respect to the levels of social trust, there tends to be a minimal level of 'surface' social trust that facilitates moral sensibility, civility and tolerance in the public sphere, such as when in mixed and cross-community settings with individual members of the former enemy. But the deep levels of social trust required in the private sphere, where the boundaries of the trustworthy person are very closely and narrowly defined, is often restricted to friends and kin. This parallels Robert Putnam's distinction between thin and thick trust: 'Trust embedded in personal relations that are strong, frequent, and nested in wider networks is sometimes called "thick trust." On the other hand, a thinner trust in "the generalized other," like your new acquaintance from the coffee shop, also rests implicitly on some background of shared social networks and expectations of reciprocity' (2000: 136). (On the application of Putnam's writings on social capital to Northern Ireland, see Graham 2016.) Most first-generation victims are capable of surface social trust, but do not yet consider the erstwhile enemy as equivalent to the deeply trusted family member.

Surface social trust-building efforts amongst victims on a particularised basis consist of cross-community projects and befriending programmes organised by victim support groups and others, which extend the social networks of first-generation victims to include the 'other'. Surface trust on a particularised basis is a good basis to start practising social trust in public. Societies emerging out of conflict thus need to artfully and skilfully construct everyday spaces for trust building, so that networks of social trust can be built slowly and people's confidence in the reliability of people from the other community is restored. These networks of social trust require careful nurturing. They are facilitated by policies and practices in civil society – in schools, women's groups, churches, universities, trade unions, in youth groups and the like – and they are easily undermined, as people question the confidence they place in erstwhile enemies and as their sense of vulnerability increases. Politicians, governments, the media, journalists, public commentators and cultural critics, parents, priests and pastors thus need to choose their words carefully so as to support rather than undermine lay people's confidence in social trust. All too often careless use of language and senseless behaviour can erode social trust and polarise rather than heal divisions.

78 ADVANCED INTRODUCTION TO THE SOCIOLOGY OF PEACE PROCESSES

A sociology of hope

The capacity to trust is linked to the capacity to hope, that is, to the anticipation of a better future. This implicates a sociology of hope and here I wish to extend my previous work on the sociology of hope (Brewer 2010: 125–31, 2018b: 249–50). Hope is inherently a forward-focused emotion. This is precisely why it is ignored in most literature on victims. Transitional justice experts neglect hope because of the concept's unfortunate connection with religious eschatology and end-times thinking, and public discourse overlooks it because public discourse prioritises past-focused emotions. This disregard is despite the fact that there is a global discourse of hope by governments and corporations. The universality of the discourse on hope calls for a proper sociological understanding of the concept.

As Bar-Tal (2001) noted with respect to Israel–Palestine, collective fear can dominate people's emotional repertoire in situations of intractable conflict and prevent the development of hope. For this reason, peace processes require an envisioning of the future as much as an emotional packaging of the past. The likelihood of travails during peace processes obliges the need for a vision to sustain people. Hope, in other words, is as critical as shame–guilt. However, hope is not enough on its own without the conditions to sustain it. Psychologists define hope in personal terms as the ability to formulate achievable goals (Bandura 1989; Stotland 1969), which makes it more than just wishing or optimism, recognising that hope will be reducible to wishful thinking unless the means are perceived by which the goals can be attained (Burnett and Maruna 2004: 395). Even so, the emphasis is upon perception – people envisioning means and ends – making hope a cognitive process. It can easily become a circular argument when couched in these terms: those people who succeed in achieving their goals were the ones with the cognitive processing skills called hope.

A sociological definition of hope is thus needed. Sociologically we can see hope as a double emotion, with associated performative behaviours. Hope has two qualities: *hoping*, the act of imagining a future desirable set of social circumstances, and the ways to get there (that is, it supplies a secular eschatology), and *anticipation*, the internal feelings excited by the desirable end state being envisioned (that is, it provokes other future-focused emotions). Hoping and anticipation are indivisible, for the wished-for end state has to be one that is longed for, one that involves feelings of excitement and anticipation; only people outside the normal social bonds hope for something undesirable to happen to the social group and get excited by anticipating harm. This is why it is better to see hope as two complementary emotions rather than one – hoping-anticipation. Linking anticipating with hoping in this way explains why hope is inherently positive and forward looking; no religious eschatology is needed to associate it inevitably with progress and optimism.

In sociology, furthermore, hope is also a public emotion not restricted to the private sphere, in that cultural values can shape what is collectively hoped for and how it is achieved. Its *publicness* is obvious. It is an emotion affected by social conditions, something that can be constructed for societal goals by means of social change in the conditions that sustain it, with people's private perceptions open to management, to enable the collectivity to imagine a desirable future and the means to achieve it. Hope and social change are thus in a symbiotic relationship. Social change is important to creating the conditions for sustaining hoping-anticipating, while hoping-anticipating helps bring about social change. Hope's envisioning of social change in the future, for example, may in situations of social conflict involve anticipating the ending of killings, but also new identities, new political regimes and new forms of social relations.

There are various social practices, technologies and social policies for this purpose, including museums that envision the future as much as record the past, as well as use of the education curriculum in schools, media initiatives, citizenship education programmes, public memorials and so on. Hope-anticipation is one way to harness the activism of non-governmental organisations (NGOs) and civil society groups on many issues relevant to peace processes. Various social and cultural spaces for hoping can be developed, which place people in social spaces that increase their sense of anticipation at the hoped-for end state. These can be cultural spaces, such as through poetry, drama and art exhibitions that envision a peaceful future and focus on hoping and anticipating the end state; political spaces, where groups and parties debate means–ends; religious spaces, through which the Churches and para-church organisations stress the importance of hope; and medical spaces, where welfare and medical care bring hope for health and cure, and so on. For all these reasons, while it may seem the most personal and individualised of emotions, hope is deeply sociological.

80 ADVANCED INTRODUCTION TO THE SOCIOLOGY OF PEACE PROCESSES

Conclusion

Post-conflict emotions are in the shadowlands, ignored by the sociology of emotions and viewed very selectively within transitional justice studies. The second cognitivist revolution in sociology, however, has encouraged sociology to analyse an array of seemingly personal and intimate emotions, formerly seen as the domain of humanistic disciplines, like love, hate, mercy, vulnerability, empathy, compassion, compromise, forgiveness, revenge and shame, amongst others. In so doing, sociology shows how deeply embedded these 'private' 'personal' emotions are in public behaviour and how moulded they are by social structural conditions. This second cognitivist revolution offers an opportunity and a challenge to the sociology of peace processes. The opportunity is one to explore the emotional landscape of people in societies emerging out of conflict. The challenge is to identify the range of emotions that enable or hinder the social peace process.

The sociology of emotions has yet to discover the potential of studying post-conflict emotions, so much of the discussion of emotions occurs within the discipline of transitional justice. The attention of the latter is normally on 'negative' emotions, like anger, guilt, shame and revenge. There have been a few hugely significant sociological contributions to understanding this narrow range of emotions, notably shame (for example Ray, Smith and Wastell 2004; Scheff 1994, 2000, 2011a, 2011b) and retribution (Elster 2004: 129ff.). Using the lens of the sociology of peace processes, however, we can see that not all of these emotions are 'negative', notably righteous anger. The attention given to 'positive' emotions in the transitional justice literature pales in comparison, but the sociological approach adopted here shows that some of these are dysfunctional to peace, not deserving the description of positive, notably forms of conditional two-party forgiveness. The distinction between past-focused and future-focused emotions seems a better way to contrast the array of emotions in transitioning societies, some of which look to managing the issues of the past and some towards the future; and some looking in both directions at the same time.

Past-focused emotions rooted as a legacy of violence need to be dealt with in the present. Anger, guilt, shame, remorse, hate and revenge, amongst others, can be inhibitors to peace by limiting the development of moral sensibility and social solidarity in the social peace process. By sociologically deconstructing these past-focused emotions and developing typologies of them, they are shown to be more subtle and complex than portrayed in the literature, and some of them are forward looking in their impacts on moral sensibility, civility and tolerance, assisting people in learning to live together after conflict.

Forgiveness and anger are two emotions that look backwards and forwards at the same time, and the sociology of forgiveness and the sociology of anger as developed here, highlight how some of their forms enable, some inhibit, moral sensibility in the social peace process. The future-focused emotions of mercy, social trust and hope can also be deconstructed sociologically and be shown to be identifiably forward facing. The emotional landscape of people in societies emerging out of conflict thus needs to be approached broadly, discussing not only anger, shame, revenge and the forgiveness of past wrongs, but also a new discourse of emotions promoted by the second cognitivist revolution, based around love, mercy, trust, compromise, hope, emotional empathy and reparative humanism.

The ambitions of this chapter have been simultaneously small-scale and grand. They have been small-scale because I have outlined the opportunity that the cognitivist revolution affords the sociology of peace processes to explore the emotional landscape of transitioning societies, through conceptual clarification of the emotions relevant to them rather than empirical studies of real people. The empirical research, after all, has already been done on victims (Brewer, Hayes and Teeney 2018; Brewer et al. 2018), on bystanders (Brewer and Hayes 2011b, 2013, 2015a, 2015b), and ex-combatants (Brewer 2021a, 2021c; Brewer and Wahidin 2021). The conceptual clarification in this chapter of some key post-conflict emotions, notably guilt, anger, forgiveness, mercy, trust and hope, is, on the other hand, very bold. I have challenged the representation of emotions in transitional justice studies, offered a sociological perspective on key emotions that sociology has hitherto ignored, and laid down a challenge to the sociology of emotions to begin to apply its special insights to explore post-conflict emotions.

6 The sociology of everyday life peacebuilding

Introduction

This chapter introduces the notion of everyday life peacebuilding that has recently been developed in International Relations (IR) studies. It argues that this application is severely limited by its non-sociological understanding of the term 'everyday life'. It is reduced to describing an arena in which ordinary, routine and mundane peacebuilding activities occur. This neglects sociology's most significant contribution to understanding everyday life as a concept; namely, that it is also a process of mundane reasoning. This argument is important for two reasons. First, it provides sociology with the opportunity to contribute to the inter-disciplinary field of peace studies and for the sociological imagination to finesse and clarify one of the field's newest and most innovative concepts. Second, sociological theorisation of everyday life peacebuilding connects to the emphasis in the sociology of peace processes on moral sensibility and the restoration of society after conflict through the intersubjective relational ethic that recreates sociability. This chapter thus links back to arguments in Chapter 3 and shows the interconnectedness of the themes that the sociology of peace processes champions.

After introducing the notion of everyday life peacebuilding in IR, the chapter draws on empirical data from victims of conflict in Northern Ireland, South Africa and Sri Lanka to demonstrate how victims' processes of mundane reasoning significantly add to our understanding of everyday life peacebuilding and its outcomes (an extended treatment of these issues can be found in Brewer et al. 2018: 199–254). The arguments give additional support to Neal and Murji's point (2015: 813) that ordinary everyday practices converge with, and are manifestations of, wider social forces, what Charles Tilly (1989) once referred to as the small things in big structures, large processes and huge comparisons. It is thus necessary to be disabused of the view, articulated sometimes by advocates of everyday life sociology (Adler, Adler and Fontana 1987), that it only deals with the micro. Its relevance to big issues cannot be better illustrated than by the topic of everyday life peacebuilding. First, let us consider what everyday life is sociologically.

What is everyday life?

Everyday life is a widely used term in social science with a long history, especially in sociology (Bennett and Watson 2002; Kalekin-Fishman 2013; Neal and Murji 2015; Pink 2012), although having undergone a renaissance because of its popularity in feminist research and cultural studies (Felski 1999), and its associations with public sociology activism (Pink 2012). Its rediscovery has taken it away from its roots in US micro interactionist studies of social behaviour (on which see Adler, Adler and Fontana 1987; Douglas et al. 1980) but the meaning has remained constant. Everyday life is the day-to-day, taken-for-granted, ordinary habits and routines of social life. It is the realm in which ordinary, taken-for-granted, habitual social life is performed, experienced and understood as ordinary, taken-for-granted and habitual. So important is this to the reproduction of social life that Sztompka (2008) described it as the 'third sociology' after those of order and action discussed in Chapter 2, although it is hardly a 'new turn' in the discipline as claimed.

Everyday life is not a physical space (a place) as such, in that these taken-for-granted routines occur everywhere: in the home, at work, in school, during leisure. In Erving Goffman's (1959) famous distinction, these taken-for-granted routines and habits occur both backstage, in the private sphere, and frontstage, in the public sphere, and thus everyday life transcends the public–private dichotomy. It is best to conceive of everyday life as a social space rather than an actual place (Lefebvre 2009). Social spaces are partly physical (the office, the university, the restaurant), but they are also virtual in that they transcend physical spaces to describe the realm or domain in which mundane social life is performed and experienced. Consider the everyday life of family life (Scott 2009).

84   ADVANCED INTRODUCTION TO THE SOCIOLOGY OF PEACE PROCESSES

Family life occurs sometimes in physical space (the home), but mostly in social spaces that transcend physical space. Everyday life is thus more than a physical place; it is everywhere where everyday routines, habits and taken-for-granted life are accomplished. It is therefore constituted by its own practices; it is everywhere where the ordinary is rendered as ordinary.

Three features stand out about this definition. First, everyday life is a social space where ordinariness, normality and routine are performed, existing in places but transcending all physical spaces at the same time. It is thus both *in* places but simultaneously spans *all* spaces. Second, everyday life has a temporality, in that this ordinariness is performed day after day after day. This temporality gives everyday life its regularity, habituality, predictability and taken-for-grantedness that distinguishes it and defines it as a social space. Third, everyday life is also a form of reasoning. It describes the ways of thinking which end up with ordinary people, as they go about their day-to-day habitual life, reproducing a sense of things as being routine and normal. Mundane reasoning as Pollner (1987) described it, sometimes known as common-sense reasoning (Brewer 1984), makes habitual, taken-for-granted social life seem ordinary because lay people have a mode of thinking that makes sense of the world by first rendering social life into what they take to be the normal (Pollner 1987: 33ff. illustrated it by the practical reasoning participants used in traffic courts).

It is mundane reason that recreates the everyday on a daily basis. Routine is created by our sense of the routine and the process of routinisation by which we understand the world through what is routine. Put another way, normality is constituted by the process of normalisation, our way of thinking about the world through what we take to be normal. Everyday life is therefore constituted by its own mundane reasoning practices; it is everywhere where the ordinary is rendered as ordinary and habitual, and made into the taken-for-granted routines through which everything we think about what is ordinary and is thus made ordinary.

Mundane reason is different from the term 'practical reasoning' as used in the philosophy of action, where practical reason describes the plan of action people use to realise their goals, contrasting with theoretical or speculative reasoning, which is sometimes called pure reason. In the sociology of everyday life, practical reasoning describes the taken-for-granted, everyday methods people use to accomplish the ordinary, routine and normal activities that comprise everyday life (Psathas 1980). This includes everyday life's practical actions, its common-sense knowledge, and its practical reasoning that employs background interpretative schemas to accomplish whatever is designed or required. We return to this definition when we explore victims' mundane reasoning. The prior question needs to be asked first. What is everyday life peacebuilding?

What is everyday life peacebuilding?

Everyday life is everywhere where taken-for-granted, ordinary habits are reproduced. There is, thus, an everyday life of politics, of market trading, of government decision-making, of shopping and, indeed, of family life (on the latter, see Scott 2009). There is also an everyday life of peacebuilding, like there is an everyday life of all things that reproduce ordinary, habitual and taken-for-granted routines. To consider peacebuilding as ordinary and constituted by habitual and taken-for-granted practices is the new and recent discovery of IR. What everyday life peacebuilding means to one of the most prolific and finest IR scholars, Roger Mac Ginty (2014), is bottom-up, local agency by ordinary people rather than top-down so-called track-one diplomacy. Mac Ginty and Richmond (2013) refer to this as 'the local turn' in peacebuilding. It is the everyday, almost banal 'conflict-calming' measures that people routinely engage in locally. This approach is not without its critics precisely because it challenges orthodoxy (for example Dzuverovic 2021; Paffenhalz 2015) but it has provoked considerable scholarship in IR (for a review of the literature on the 'local turn' see Leonardsson and Rudd 2015).

In Mac Ginty's approach, this bottom-up local agency by ordinary people in conflict societies achieves two ends: they are the practices that help people negotiate their way through life in the midst of the conflict in order to cope with and adjust to it; and they are the conflict-calming practices they employ in this process that end up reducing conflict in their ordinary lives. Drawing on his own experiences growing up in Northern Ireland during 'the Troubles', he focuses on those numbers of lay people who navigate their way through the conflict and engage in conflict-calming practices. Mac Ginty lists some of these practices (2014: 555–7), distinguishing between: *avoidance* strategies (avoiding contentious topics of conversation, avoiding offensive displays, forms of escapism and withdrawal); strategies for constructing *ambiguity* (concealing identity markers, dissembling in speech and actions); practices for *ritualised politeness* (manners, civility, tolerance); forms of *blame deferral* (blaming outsiders and external forces); and strategies for risk management through *telling* (use of socially learned behaviours that 'tell' identity in order to manage risky and threatening people and situations).

The notion of the everyday that is embedded in this approach portrays it as the normal habitus of individuals and groups, in which the familiar is reproduced as familiar and normal. It is thus constituted as a sphere (what he calls the 'informal sphere') *and* as a set of everyday practices (that reproduce civility and construct conflict avoidance and conflict calming by using the above strategies and practices).

Sociology has a lot to contribute to this debate. The problem with the idea of everyday life peacebuilding as conceived in Mac Ginty's approach reflects the disciplinary closure through which the concept of everyday life is understood. Understood within IR, everyday life is reduced to the idea of local spaces and local practices. This seriously underplays its nature and limits its peacebuilding potential, overlooking the way in which everyday life is also a mode of reasoning by which the mundane is reproduced as normal and routine. Sociology's contribution is the idea that everyday life practices of peacebuilding are embedded in everyday reasoning processes that reproduce peace as an everyday practice. By breaking down the boundaries between the disciplines and exploring sociology's understanding of the concept of everyday life, we can see that sociology can both add to the understanding of the nature of everyday life peacebuilding and address its weaknesses. Substantiating this claim in the next section with data from victims in Northern Ireland, South Africa and Sri Lanka brings us to the apex of my argument in this chapter.

Mundane reasoning and everyday life peacebuilding

Mundane reasoning encourages ways of thinking about the victimhood experience that have implications for victims' capacity to learn to live together with moral sensibility, tolerance and civility after conflict. I emphasise the following features about victims' mundane reasoning

THE SOCIOLOGY OF EVERYDAY LIFE PEACEBUILDING   87

that help reproduce everyday life peacebuilding: (1) victims' reproduction of normal routines; (2) victims' ways of thinking about non-competitive victimhood; (3) victims' ways of thinking about social relations and the necessity for cross-community engagement with the erstwhile other; (4) their ways of thinking about the necessity of forward-focused emotions; and (5) their ways of thinking about the importance of 'getting along' after conflict.

These mundane reasoning practices deconstruct an otherwise important distinction in the philosophy of action between 'instrumental practical reasoning' and 'value-oriented practical reasoning'. This owes much to the sociologist Max Weber's distinction between forms of rationality (Weber 1968 [1921]). Two of Weber's types are relevant to this discussion. Weber refers to instrumental rationality, where actors are oriented to achieve an instrumental end, and value rationality, where actors are oriented to realise ethical and moral ends (Kalberg 1980). Within these five modes of mundane reasoning victims display both an orientation to the instrumental goals to be achieved through it *and* to the moral and ethical values which they practise by it. They were both instrumental and value oriented in their mundane reasoning, looking to achieve concrete practical ends and realise ethical goals.

I illustrate these modes of mundane reasoning with extracts of anonymised data from the Leverhulme study of victims in Northern Ireland, South Africa and Sri Lanka (see Brewer, Hayes and Teeney 2018; Brewer et al. 2018).

1.   Reproduction of normal routines

The maintenance of the everyday day life routines that constituted pre-victimhood normality got quickly reasserted. Comfort, perhaps even healing, was found in the old routines and they were reproduced within the constraints of the mental and physical harm that victimhood brought. That is to say, victims constituted a 'new normal' consistent with these constraints that reproduced the everyday life routines that defined their everyday life to the fullest extent that victimhood permitted. As one Northern Irish respondent said: 'you just focused on the daily routine. Keeping things as normal as can be in a situation like that.' The reproduction of everyday routines and ways of thinking became a coping mech-

88   ADVANCED INTRODUCTION TO THE SOCIOLOGY OF PEACE PROCESSES

anism that restored a sense of 'new normality'. Another Northern Irish victim described the comfort he found in doing ordinary routines again:

> I went to my GP and he prescribed medication, which I took for a day and realised that this was more delusion. I started swimming, I started running, I started trying to be a better father to my kids. And in some respects, I stopped feeling sorry for myself. Very fortunate that I had a good job too. Good summer holidays. Slowly but surely the old spark came back.

'You just kept going', another victim said, 'it was just part of life now'. This way of thinking about their victimhood made the 'new normal' normal. Inherent in its normality were other interpretative schema that rebuilt sociability.

2.   Ways of thinking about non-competitive victimhood

This manifests itself in the emotional empathy extended to victims from the 'other side' and in some cases, the emotional empathy victims extend to their attacker. The latter is clearly the more difficult for victims. In Northern Ireland, for example, many victims believed that any person in need, regardless of their past, should receive the help they require. The needs of people with injuries should be met regardless of their political or personal background, without distinction between victim and perpetrator. This is expressed well in the following extract:

> The term hierarchy of victims is used quite a lot. As far as I am concerned they shouldn't be. When you see the services and the help, initially, it tended to go towards the security forces. As far as I am concerned, if a policeman lost both legs and I lost both legs, we both need the same service and we both need the same help. Perpetrators, they are always putting a spanner in the spokes whenever you are trying to move forward. But my argument would be, if people are in need. You find that a lot of people that have been injured, and they are a perpetrator – I don't think there are that many to tell you the truth. I know there is a few that lost an arm planting a bomb and nearly died in the process as well. If they are in need yes. I think that if they are in need people should get help. If we are moving forward as a society you cannot start judging people on what they did. I definitely feel like that. Certainly their needs should be met. From my own point of view, it is based on if you need something.

A young Catholic victim disabled by Loyalist gunmen in a case of mistaken identity, extended this generosity to his attackers: 'I can't even blame the young men that shot me. They thought that they were doing their best for Ulster and God and all the rest of it.'

THE SOCIOLOGY OF EVERYDAY LIFE PEACEBUILDING   89

Thinking of your erstwhile enemy as a victim much like yourself is a form of mundane reasoning critical to the development on non-competitive forms of victimhood in which moral sensibility is embedded in everyday life. In South Africa, in some of the victims who were enthused with a sense of common humanity, there was an emotional empathy with their former Afrikaans oppressor, seeing them also as victims of British colonialism: 'When I started looking at things, and I started reading and researching, and then I started looking at what the British did to the Afrikaner'.

Former political prisoners interviewed in South Africa spoke of the importance of their imprisonment for the development of a more inclusive approach to victimhood. The following extract describes how an apartheid victim changed his way of thinking once he was exposed to what he called the 'ANC university' on Robben Island:

> When I got to [Robben] Island I was an ill-disciplined young man. And the elderly comrades took me under their wings, and started to teach me, this is not the way things are done, and so on. And then we got involved in political discussions, and the history of the ANC, and global politics and all that. And there the ANC taught you, it is not the white people that's the problem. It is the system, it is there that the problem lies. So there you learnt that it is not about yourself, it is about taking your country forward.

The double victimhood of Tamils in Sri Lanka, reflected in personal injury and defeat as a vanquished group, might be thought to render this form of mundane reasoning very difficult for Tamils. Sinhalese respondents, as the victors, were frequent in espousing it. For example, one said:

> We cannot say it was only the Sinhalese who were most affected by the war. During the cessation of hostilities, we visited Jaffa. Then we met the refugees of war at the refugee camp at school. There were refugees in the place whose situation was much worse than that of ours. For we became helpless only from one side; namely, from the LTTE [Liberation Tigers of Tamil Eelam] attacks only. The Sri Lankan army did not oppress us, the Sinhalese. But the Tamils had to suffer from two sides; namely, the LTTE on one side and the Sri Lankan army on the other, who would confront Tamil people with death threats if their children had joined the LTTE. But the Tamil children joined the LTTE not out of free will, but those were forcefully conscripted.

This mode of reasoning enabled Sinhala victims to realise the extent of Tamil suffering. What is significant is that Tamils also expressed an overwhelming commitment to inclusive ways of thinking about their victimhood. Mundane reasoning resulted in inclusive views of the other that was the key to their emotional progress. As a Tamil Catholic woman remarked, 'my husband died due to the war, and I will not gain anything if I remain angry with people who killed my husband. So, it is better to forgive the murderers.' In this form of reasoning there is tension caused by the need to forgive the unforgivable. This tension is expressed succinctly by the following Tamil Hindu mother: 'We have the feeling that we suffered a lot due to the war. So, we have ill-feelings towards the other ethnic group. My son died due to shelling, so I am unable to forgive the one responsible for that, but still, I have to forgive and start my new life all over again.' A Catholic Tamil said: 'Without any conditions I can forgive the people responsible for my victimhood because there is no point in talking about the past. We, all the people in the country, should live happily and peacefully.' In fact, one Catholic Tamil said that the scale of the atrocities made it easier to forgive, since bad things happen in war: 'If it is in the context of war, I should forgive, it is easier to forgive in the context of war. We have to understand the nature of the war.'

3.   Ways of thinking about social relations

Social relations refers to ways of thinking about the erstwhile other that implicate recognition of the importance of rebuilding relationships through cross-community engagement and networks. One victim in Northern Ireland commented positively on their experiences with a cross-community group: 'We have gone cross-community, which I would not have done. This group has brought me to that stage. It is not the government. It is my own understanding. Because I do not want my grandchildren to go through what my children went through in "the Troubles" and all.' The phrase 'it is my own understanding' comes nearest to expressing this woman's own realisation that it is her ways of thinking about the importance of garnering social relations with the erstwhile enemy that have driven her to engage in cross-community engagement. 'Saying things to yourself' serves as the equivalent realisation for the following victim: 'It was brilliant. We were able to go down and we met women from down the South of Ireland, and you listened to their stories. So, I think the more you hear from other people as well the more you can relate to them. And you can say to yourself – they are just like us as well. And people can set aside their differences then.' Ways of thinking about the other that predicate new everyday social relationships, encourage changed social networks, which can further consequences for inclusive social relations. For example, some Northern Irish victims reported that their children now had friends or partners from the 'other community'. As one Catholic victim said, 'our children now, we have a daughter who is going with a Protestant and another grandchild who is going with a Protestant.'

In South Africa, some of our participants consciously sought social connectedness across racial boundaries in order to mirror Nelson Mandela's new 'rainbow nation' in their everyday social relationships, thinking that the rainbow nation was a personal obligation as much as a political slogan. 'I have a lot of friends that are pastors', one said, 'white pastors, and we try to break the barriers between the Christians. We started a team, a soccer team, and I have white friends who have joined our churches and we have sports together, playing together and eating together. That I think is bringing healing to the other people. Because I myself am healed.'

Social connectedness of this kind was rarely possible in apartheid South Africa, except perhaps within the anti-apartheid movement itself. However, the end of apartheid has not on the whole meant that most people's social networks now include people from other 'race groups'. The notable exception is middle-class professionals in specific inter-racial urban neighbourhoods. For our respondents, the lack of racial integration remains an important obstacle to genuine reconciliation. As a result, social connectedness is little different now than during the apartheid era. This is important in that it impacts on mundane reasoning practices in ways that restrict the new social relations that can build social trust and respect. It is also critical because it is in these mixed networks and friendship groups in everyday life that experiences of the past are spoken about, and new memories are constituted.

With respect to Sri Lanka, where opportunities for inclusive and integrated social relations are greater than in post-apartheid South Africa, a Sinhalese interviewee in rural north-central Sri Lanka affirmed how their thoughts about Tamils changed when they attended a cross-community reconciliation workshop that encouraged new ways of thinking:

> When we spoke to them [Tamils] we found that they had suffered more than we did. We had gone to a workshop of Sarvodhaya [a local NGO]. They organized workshops. I went with three others from the village. There were Sinhalese, Tamil and Muslim people. No religious or ethnic differences. We also attended the workshops organized by the World Vision – workshops

for peace, reconciliation. When we considered their [Tamils] troubles, it was useless asking them to live in brotherhood with us. Now we can. Why we say that now we can, is they come to our village as well. They [Tamils] come and buy cow dung. Now we are not afraid as we did earlier. Those days we were afraid of people who came to collect used tins and irons as well. We feared that they were spies. We were suspicious of those people. Maybe they were spies or maybe not, but we suspected them. Now speaking about compromise, I do not know about others, I think they have a reason to hate us.

Participation in mixed social networks allows Sri Lankan victims to see their common experiences, changing their ways of thinking about victimhood. As one Sinhalese respondent admitted, 'they [Tamils] are also at the same level. When we talk to them, we get the impression that among them also there are those who are under adverse psychological effects.'

4.   Ways of thinking about future-focused emotions

Future-focused emotions means recognition at the level of everyday life reasoning of the importance of moving on, of having hope for the future, and of not letting the past keep you locked there. Of course, very few victims want to or are able to forget the past but thinking about the future is an important component of their mundane reasoning. In Northern Ireland, many victims in the sample argued that the way to think about the past is to couple it with the future, so that they both remember and forget; remembering the past but only to the extent that it does not hinder moving on. The majority welcome the idea of remembrance in a historical or educational context, and while the format of *how* to represent the past was an issue to them, nearly all Northern Irish respondents reported to have moved on themselves and felt society should do so too. This connection between personal and social hope in their mundane reasoning is critical; thinking about the importance of personal growth allows society to grow: 'I think we need to move on. I think we need to move on, and we need to stop all this. I know that people say that they want Enquiries, and they want justice and things like that. But I think it is to me to draw a line under it and start trying to build the country for the kids and the people now.' 'I don't think they should forget about it. They can't let it drag them down. They have to move on. Obviously, you can't forget about loved ones, and some of the atrocities. But you do have to move on.' Northern Ireland would be a better place, one said, if people 'could all let go of the past'.

It was clear that some respondents had a form of mundane reasoning that was oriented towards the future. Interviewees wanted everyday problems and issues to be dealt with, but the anticipation and hoping was for a normal society with normal politics. Some of the Northern Irish victims were victimised a considerable time ago, and their thoughts about the future may have become more hopeful over the years, yet they reported that their views had not changed. For whatever reason, moving on was thought to be critical for themselves as well as for Northern Ireland. One victim linked this to forgiveness: 'You have to learn to forgive, or you won't move on.'

Forgiveness is one of the post-conflict emotions that looks backward and forward simultaneously. This is captured well by Northern Irish victims. Forgiveness was recognised by many respondents as the key to releasing the hold the past had on them, permitting movement forward to the future. That is to say, mundane reasoning processes linked their inheritance of the future to releasing the past through the practice of forgiveness. A significant number of Northern Irish interviewees even said they had forgiven their former perpetrators. This is despite the realisation that by forgiving perpetrators, victims take on some of the emotional burden that perpetrators are released of through forgiveness: 'I am taking on their burden. I am taking something away from them. That they can stand up and say – well I met [name deleted] and [name deleted] shook my hands and says that he forgave me for killing his [deleted].' As we have already seen, often these accounts were characterised by victims empathising with the circumstances that led ordinary people much like themselves to become perpetrators in the first place, blaming the circumstances at the time, rather than blaming the actual perpetrator: 'For me to forgive I would have to hold them to blame. And they were doing what they thought was right and I was doing what I thought was right.'

This future orientation in victims' mundane reasoning was not as evident in South Africa, where hopes for the future are negatively affected by continued social injustice. One staff member of the Truth and Reconciliation Commission commented on the link many victims make between forgiveness and social justice in their everyday reasoning practices:

> I see this, even if I think about victims, and people ask victims 'have you forgiven the perpetrator?' What I see with victims is that they have moments. And maybe after the amnesty hearing when they heard the perpetrator confess, they felt a bit better about it. And then later on as they see the perpetrator goes

94   ADVANCED INTRODUCTION TO THE SOCIOLOGY OF PEACE PROCESSES

on and continues to become a wealthy businessman and they are still living in poverty, their feelings change. So, there is this notion that it is an absolute condition, to me it waxes and wanes.

Nonetheless, there are many magnanimous gestures of forgiveness in apartheid victims (a point made long ago by Gobodo-Madikizela 2008):

> What they did to us, we forgive them. As a Muslim and also as Christian, we believe God forgives. Don't we? And I will ask myself who am I not to forgive. Now this is a very good example: if you take Mandela, he was in prison for 27 years, and he was released in 1990. He could have declared war. But he said to the National Party: I don't hate you; I forgive you for what you did to me.

The link between forgiveness and moving on from the past was raised several times by South African respondents. In their reasoning processes moving on was not equated with forgetting. One apartheid victim put it like this: 'If you hurt me a lot, I will be with you and I will forgive, but I will not forget what you have done.' Another said: 'You are not going to forget, but you would rather forgive. Otherwise, you are going to make a wreck of yourself.' In apartheid victims' ways of thinking about the past and the future, many hold them in tandem. One respondent used the metaphor of the mythical Sankofa bird that flies with its head backward to highlight that it is important to look to the future but acknowledge the past: 'we need to know where we come from in order to know where we are going. So, you have to combine these things constantly.' Modes of mundane reasoning about the past–future relationship are therefore pragmatic, thinking it unhealthy to overly live in the past: 'I don't want to think the back way because then I am going to get sick.'

Actively working at not 'thinking back' has parallels with what I call 'remembering forwards' (Brewer 2020) as a release from the hold of the past, allowing some apartheid victims to make a link in their mundane reasoning between leaving the past behind and progressing in life. As one respondent said: 'Of course, there are instances when you remember things in the past and you feel like, if it had not been for the apartheid government, I would not be where I am today. Maybe that's where the victimhood comes in. But of course, one tries hard not to really dwell on that. Because dwelling on that really keeps back one's progress in life.'

Some victims in Sri Lanka also spoke of the need to move on and located their practice of forgiveness in this context, thinking of forgiveness as

THE SOCIOLOGY OF EVERYDAY LIFE PEACEBUILDING   95

a prerequisite to moving forward. Forgiveness was thus a way of managing past-focused anger and a facilitation to thinking about the future. Mundane reasoning processes like this are forward-focused in their emotional empathy. As one Sri Lankan said, 'several innocent lives have been wasted for nothing. People were killed or died for no reason whatsoever. But we should forgive and move forward.' The challenge with respect to forgiveness of the near unforgivable is summarised well in this victim's witness. By not forgiving them, victims remain frozen in the moment of their victimhood, consumed by the anger and unable to move on. Forgiveness is thus seen by many victims in their mundane reasoning processes as the key to their emotional progress. As a Tamil Catholic woman remarked, 'my husband died due to the war, and I will not gain anything if I remain angry with people who killed my husband. So, it is better to forgive the murderers.' It is not just Tamil Catholics who articulated such magnanimity. A Sinhala Buddhist woman said: 'No, can't keep hatred always in your heart. Our son when this father was hospitalised, held my hand and said I will join the army one day. I asked why, and he said that it was they [the LTTE] who placed the bomb that injured father. At that time I said, son, do not think that way.'

5.   Ways of thinking about 'getting along'

I have deliberately left until last one of the most significant dimensions of everyday life mundane reasoning since it connects to the dominant emphasis in the sociology of peace processes on the rediscovery of moral sensibility by the practice of the intersubjective relational ethic that restores sociability after conflict. As discussed in Chapter 3, this relational ethic reproduced society after the ruins of conflict. Here I wish to locate the ethic in the mundane reasoning practices of victims that generate their minimum moral standard that says their victimhood should not happen again, or happen to others, especially not their children and grandchildren. This is a way of thinking that prioritises 'getting along' after conflict for the sake of reproducing sociability itself. As a Tamil in Sri Lanka said, 'we are grown up people and we have led our lives and ours was the period of struggle and turbulence, at least if our children and children's children can be happy that would be a great relief.' A Protestant respondent in Northern Ireland said much the same, even if only more fulsomely:

I have moved on from [my victimhood]. We have friends now who are Catholics, and we get on very well with them. You empathise with them, and you sort of understand. And you do understand what they went through, what their families went through and what they have went through and that gives you a bond, more so than I would think any religion would give you. Because you do understand. Everybody bleeds the same and everybody hurts the same.

Enhanced emotional empathy, garnered in this case through mundane reasoning that sees victimhood as a shared experience, reduced the de-humanisation of people from the other community, and was an important factor in restoring sociability with the erstwhile 'other'. There seems a minimum moral baseline not to let their children and grandchildren go through the same experiences and suffering. This motivation was very strong:

Well, I don't think that we are going to get anywhere without [compromise]. There has to be compromise, give and take or whatever, on both sides. As I say maybe 30 or 40 years ago compromise wouldn't have been a word I would have even entertained. If somebody had said to me, look we are going to have to compromise here if we are going to move forward. It just would have been basically 'F... you and your compromise, it ain't going to happen as far as I am concerned.' But as I say now, I will be approaching 60 next year, I think you are thinking changes radically and I think there has to be a lot of compromise on both, if we ever. My sons are from their mid-20s up. I have grandchildren, I have a load of grandchildren I will give you some if you want. I don't want my grandchildren going through all this again.

South Africans readily accepted that their political settlement involved compromises that were necessary for the sake of getting along. As one apartheid victim commented:

We were [...] disappointed with the kind of deal that was struck, with the sunset clause giving the oppressors opportunities and rights to continue beyond our liberation to still be in charge of the economy, to still be in charge of land rights and so on. So it was a major compromise right from the outset. So, we had a compromised victory, and an agreement, and the peace accord was that central document in 1991/92, that determined those particular kinds of processes and how we were going to be liberated, and form part of this democracy.

Though characterised as 'sell out' by a small number, compromise was also identified by a far greater number as 'reaching a political solution in the interest of the greater good', and as such was necessary at the time. Disappointed expectations about social transformation now cloud the view of some: 'I think in the beginning it was a good compromise. Because we did not know, we did not understand, because we fought for the freedom of our country, and to vote and to be free, and to use all the facilities of our country. And I think we actually in terms of that particular fight, we won that particular fight, but in terms of economic freedom, we did not receive that.' This mundane reasoning that thinks of compromise as a necessary bargain, was expressed in many of the South African interviews: 'Compromise was necessary, because what alternatives were there? We could have an armed struggle, we could have had a civil war. There are many examples in the world where people fight until there is no infrastructure left. So much damage done that you can't rebuild. So we were in a situation, objectively, where the compromise was the only option.'

Practical reasoning and discordant accounts

As Goffman reminds us, the self is always open to being discredited; so too the self's accounts. A key sociological question thus arises at this juncture about victims' mundane reasoning. How did victims deal with the realisation that other victims were not moral beacons and gave discrediting accounts that undermined their own empathetic ones? Pollner (1987: 35ff.) addressed how mundane reasoners deal with idealisations and schemes of interpretation that discredit their version of reality and how they reconciled different accounts. He refers to this as the 'self-preservation of mundane reason' (1987: 48ff.). He argues that mundane reason provides its own grounds for this reconciliation (1987: 53). By the application of common-sense practical reasoning, mundane reasoners believe that if all things are equal, persons observing the same social world will produce corroborating accounts. When this is not so, things are perceived to be unequal (1987: 65). This is the clue to victims' practical reasoning that explained away potentially discordant and discrediting accounts.

When victims are confronted with evidence in their everyday lives that clearly shows some victims whom they interact with do not share their stock of common-sense knowledge and have different beliefs, maxims, interpretative schema and typologies, it is not the validity of the assumption that victims share a common stock of knowledge that is questioned but the personal experiences of the discordant victim. The essential intersubjectivity of the victim experience is not held in doubt but personal reasons are invoked to explain away the discrediting account. The discordant accounts are rendered as untypical of victimhood generally.

ADVANCED INTRODUCTION TO THE SOCIOLOGY OF PEACE PROCESSES

Respondents in the Leverhulme study (see Brewer et al. 2018: 217–18), for example, called upon mundane reasoning to argue that the discrediting account of other victims was because they had not 'moved on', were frozen in a victim identity, disengaged from cross-community networks, were socially isolated and withdrawn, and the like. The common reality of the victimhood experience remained intact; victims with discordant accounts got explained away by mundane reasoning about their personal biography.

Conclusion

Important as victims' sense of routinisation was to its accomplishment after conflict, enabling what passed for normal to be reintroduced because of the reassurance of a sense of routine, the primary contribution of victims' mundane reasoning to peacebuilding was the new ways of thinking about their victimhood that implicated moral sensibility, the effect of which was to restore sociability. The mundane reasoning processes that generate sociability relate to the new concept of everyday life peacebuilding in significant ways. Mundane reasoning ends up in patterns of behaviour that are the very forms of everyday life peacebuilding people like Mac Ginty and others have identified as its distinguishing feature. If everyday life peacebuilding is a set of practices that take place in everyday life spheres and spaces, these practices are themselves embedded in the mundane reasoning processes that create the relational ethic of sociability as a motivation for victims to want to practise them. Engagement in cross-community initiatives, the use of conflict resolution or avoidance strategies, and participation in 'communities of compromise', are everyday life peacebuilding practices that are the outworkings of victims' relational ethic that wants them to make post-conflict society better for the sake of their children and grandchildren. This ethic is itself the outcome of victims' mundane reasoning processes.

Having established the concept's root in sociological theorising about mundane reasoning, I want to close by reflecting on everyday life peacebuilding as a form of peacebuilding. It has profound implications for what peacebuilding means. In the midst of the travails of a peace process, peace can be taken-for-granted. Peace has to be enacted anew in every generation, in every year and every day, in the living relationships of person to person in all social forums and institutions. Peacebuilding is a daily practice rooted in the mundane reasoning practices that privilege and prioritise the very set of ordinary, habitual practices that constitute its distinctiveness.

This means we have to rethink what peace competences are. 'Peace competencies' are no longer restricted to narrow sets of skills possessed by professionals but are disseminated to ordinary people in their everyday lives as part of their daily activities. Responsibility for peacebuilding is not delegated to politicians, to the conflict resolution industry or peace specialists and experts; it is everyone's responsibility to practise peace in their everyday life, building peace from the bottom up through ordinary everyday life practices. These everyday practices include the avoidance of hate speech, passing negative commentary on others' hate speech, the practice of tolerance towards others, the practice of respect for difference and diversity, taking the leap of trust, engaging others who are different in conversation, overcoming fear, demonstrating love and grace, performing acts of compromise and acts of forgiveness, applying fairness rules in the management of one's own anger, respecting others' human dignity, taking seriously the perspective of others, their language and their culture, and so on. In this way, peace is underpinned through people's daily everyday lives. Of course, peacebuilding is anchored in institutions – police, security forces, law, parliament, human rights bodies – but it also needs to be anchored in the everyday practices of ordinary people as they go about their daily lives.

What begins, therefore, with personal responsibility to engage in everyday peace practices in ordinary, daily life, can end up through processes of common-sense reasoning, with shared and common maxims, beliefs and idealisations that respect peace and moral sensibility, and restore sociability. Therefore, a sociological approach to everyday life peacebuilding does more than minimise the effects of the conflict through routine practices of everyday conflict-calming strategies. It isolates forms of mundane reasoning that can positively impact on how people coming out of conflict think about the conflict, how they understand the 'other', how they think about the relationship between the past and the future, and how they envision a shared future. In short, the sociology of everyday life peacebuilding helps us change what we think of as peace.

7 Notes towards a sociology of personal trauma

Introduction

This chapter introduces a sociological perspective on personal trauma following conflict. Personal trauma is primarily approached through the disciplines of psychology, psychotherapy and psychoanalysis, where it is medicalised, giving us conditions like post-traumatic stress disorder and post-traumatic growth. Sociology has had constructive engagements with psychoanalysis through the Frankfurt School, and particularly Erich Fromm's sociology (McLaughlin 2021), but they diverge on how they approach trauma. The pioneering work of Ron Eyerman (2012), Jeffrey Alexander (2012) and his colleagues (Alexander et al. 2004), which Woods (2019) describes as a new research paradigm, represents a sociological intervention in this hegemony by focusing on cultural trauma, the real or imagined trauma experienced by groups, feelings of which are manufactured or mobilised to mediate group relations (Eyerman 2012 and Smelser 2004 both contrast psychotherapeutic and cultural approaches to trauma). To distinguish their disciplinary approach, they often refer to personal trauma as psychological trauma. With cultural trauma attention is placed on the sociological processes through which these real or imagined traumatic experiences are disseminated culturally within the group to enhance its competitive advantage and to structure group relations.

This chapter offers a different sociological approach by addressing personal rather than group trauma after conflict, developing a perspective which locates the individual's traumatic experiences in sociological processes, the solution to which is also correspondingly sociological. It thus disputes the idea that personal trauma is psychology's exclusive domain.

The chapter develops its sociological approach to personal trauma by isolating a category of victim that is particularly subjected to traumatic hauntings, which it calls 'hidden victims'. It identifies different types of hidden victim and relates some of these types to post-colonial silencing practices. The chapter distinguishes between *silence*, and its types, and *silencing*, as an 'othering' process. Silencing is linked to power relations, including cultural, patriarchal, political and economic power, brought into particularly high relief in post-conflict and post-colonial settings. The close connection between hidden victims and inter-generational traumatic hauntings is drawn through a discussion of the moral obligation subsequent generations feel to overcome the hidden nature of their family's victimhood and to break the silencing. Truth recovery is particularly important to this process and thus the issue of who has control over truth disclosure is directly relevant to discussions of inter-generational trauma. Post-conflict and post-colonial power relations can limit truth recovery, reproducing the process of silencing and maintaining the hiddenness of some victims, perpetuating inter-generational trauma in a repetitive cycle. I do not wish to contrast this approach to that of psychotherapy and psychoanalysis, but it is worth stressing its difference with the sociology of cultural trauma.

The sociology of cultural trauma

The intense public attention on post-traumatic stress disorder seems to suggest that trauma is a recent discovery, but it has ancient origins (Caruth 1996; Leys 2000) and is now commonly discussed as part of the emotional landscape of societies emerging out of conflict. Trauma is thus one of the realities that a sociology of peace processes needs to conceptualise. The term means an injury or wound to the mind (Caruth 1996: 3–4), with long aftereffects that impact identity, memory and behaviour, which is why many writers evoke the notion of ghostly haunting to describe its consequences down the generations (see, for example, Wale, Gobodo-Madikizela and Prager 2020; Schwab 2010). This wound can be real or imagined, with the social suffering that lies behind it genuine or exaggerated. Rarely, however, is it completely fabricated, despite the

102 ADVANCED INTRODUCTION TO THE SOCIOLOGY OF PEACE PROCESSES

evocation in some cases of very long distant historical imagined hurts, for there is always some powerful and shocking occurrence behind it that mobilises opinions and emotions (Eyerman 2012). It is also inherently retrospective, relating to events in the past that are reinterpreted after the passage of time or which surface only sometime later when contemporary events help make them visible. As an example of the latter, Butalia (2000) shows that women's experiences of gendered violence in India's partition only surfaced with the emergence of the feminist movement in India nearly half a century later. This is why the psychoanalytic notion of repression is still relevant to a sociology of cultural trauma.

Cultural traumas are those real or imagined hurts that are socially constructed into traumas by the group for purposes that serve the group's interests in the present. As Smelser (2004: 35) reminds us, no historical event automatically qualifies as a cultural trauma, and the range of events that may become cultural traumas is enormous. Nonetheless, Smelser argued that societies emerging from conflict are more prone to cultural trauma. It is easy to envisage why this is the case. They are more likely to have unstable social structures, weak senses of social solidarity, and be wracked with absolutist zero-sum social cleavages around which conflict still adheres. In the language of Chapter 3, they are post-conflict societies that have retained their territorial integrity, but experience marked relational distance. The memory of real or imagined social suffering is made more culturally relevant in this context because it violates something the group holds as sacred and enforces upon group members a sense of disgust, humiliation, shame or guilt (Smelser 2004: 36). The trauma, in other words, constitutes a threat to the group and its culture, and is used to mobilise resentments and hurts in the present. This results in history having an enduring relevance that shapes group relations and can even sustain senses of revenge. Cultural traumas thus intersect with a group's social memory, in which the past is selectively remembered, to powerfully affect identity in the here-and-now (on social memory, see Misztal 2003; Sturken 1997; Urry 1996). This furnishes Alexander's (2004: 1) definition of cultural trauma. It occurs 'when members of a collectivity feel they have been subjected to a horrendous event that leaves indelible marks upon their group consciousness, marking their memories forever and changing their future identity'.

The social construction of cultural trauma relates to the idea of 'chosen trauma', an idea developed by the Turkish psychoanalyst Vamik Volkan

NOTES TOWARDS A SOCIOLOGY OF PERSONAL TRAUMA 103

(2001) to refer to groups who represent past hurts as enduring traumatic hauntings. Cultural traumas, of course, are also real rather than chosen, and Alexander and colleagues widely address the Holocaust (Alexander et al. 2004) and Svasek (2005) focuses on populations subjected to forced relocation, but Volkan (2001), perhaps with Armenian claims in mind, focuses on how groups manipulate alleged past traumas for contemporary effect. He emphasises two purposes. The 'reparative' type uses the traumatic event to unite the group and solidify its identity without harming another group. The 'destructive' type uses the chosen trauma to increase the group's sense of victimisation, to vilify a real or imagined enemy, and to resurrect dormant ideologies that claim privilege in group competition and endorse revenge.

As I have argued elsewhere (Brewer 2010: 142–4) a group's selective social memory is social in large part because it shapes individual memory, such that group hurts are experienced by group members as personal and group triumphs as personal aggrandisements. Cultural traumas, likewise, project suffering on to individual people, describing either the pain people feel at the group's humiliation and shame or the blame other people share for this group's hurt. Individuals, past and present, are thus implicated in the social construction of cultural trauma either because they experience the social suffering as personal or are responsible for it.

Alexander's (2004, 2012) 'social theory of cultural trauma' acknowledges its initial embodiment in personal experience and individual suffering (2012: 3–4). The 'lay theory of trauma', as he describes it, sees the trauma lying in people's reaction to the traumatic event itself. The 'psychoanalytical theory of trauma', grounds these traumatic feelings in repressed experiences within the self (2004: 5). The sociology of cultural trauma, on the other hand, explores the social processes that mediate the event and people's personal reaction to it, which constructs it into a collective trauma. The event thus may well be real (although many are exaggerated), but the social processes that construct the event into a cultural trauma are always artefacts and representations. This loses the connection between trauma and people's personal experiences. Cultural traumas are thus always taken out of private space and are imagined in the public sphere (Alexander 2004: 8), even though the motivating event might be real, since sociological processes artfully construct the event into collective trauma. 'Imagination', Alexander (2004: 9) writes, 'informs trauma construction just as much as when the reference is to something that has actu-

104 ADVANCED INTRODUCTION TO THE SOCIOLOGY OF PEACE PROCESSES

ally occurred.' Given that people's 'real' traumatic experiences are always imagined or re-imagined by others to turn them into cultural traumas, to distinguish what he calls the completely 'invented trauma', Eyerman (2012: fn. 6) uses the term 'mythical trauma', examples of which he gives as false memories of the Holocaust and of misremembered childhood abuse, although many alleged ancient hurts used in the Balkan wars after the collapse of Yugoslavia would also fit.

The sociology of cultural trauma, therefore, moves quickly away from the personal experience people can have of cultural trauma, either as its sufferers or its provocateurs, to focus on the abstract sociological processes by which it is constructed and disseminated in the public sphere. As Alexander (2012: 2) wrote, 'the cultural construction of collective trauma is fuelled by individual experiences of pain. Individual suffering is of extraordinary human, moral and intellectual import; in itself, however, it is a matter of ethics or psychology. My concern is with traumas that become collective.'

In this latter respect, the argument is sociologically profound. Alexander addresses how events get turned into cultural crises, so that the gap between the motivating event and its symbolic representation is filled with the 'trauma process' that involves significant carrier groups who make its meaning and who spiral its significance. This can involve a whole cultural reclassification, with new stratification hierarchies, colluded in by the state and state bureaucracies, cultural commentators, civil society groups, the media, schoolteachers and the like working in various institutional arenas, which creates a meta-narrative of cultural trauma. Even artists and performers can enact 'trauma dramas' in music, song, poetry, and in film and on stage. This meta-narrative defines the nature of the pain, identifies who are its victims and its perpetrators, and isolates the primary target audience of the narrative. The meta-narrative involves an identity revision that makes the suffering central to identity formation and it implicates new memory work that re-remembers the past and its hurts. And it is important that the meta-narrative is routinised in everyday life through what I called in Chapter 6, mundane reasoning that turns it into taken-for-granted common-sense knowledge.

Clearly, the social construction of cultural trauma takes a considerable time, well past the initial event, and a great deal needs to be achieved for cultural traumas to be experienced widely as real and to be accepted generally as such. Sometimes senses of cultural trauma are contested and are restricted to group members only (notably the claim by some Unionists that Protestants experience cultural trauma as a result of Northern Ireland's conflict), and occasionally they are disputed *within* the group as its members disagree over the extent of the harm and suffering (notably Irish revisionist historiography that disputes the negative effects of the Great Famine). Sometimes, cultural trauma can be endorsed by a new state regime that finds the cultural trauma useful for explaining the state's difficulties in implementing social and political transformation (notably South Africa, where the scale of apartheid injustices is used to explain the slow pace of change), or as a way of justifying continued repression against those alleged to be responsible for it (notably the cultural annihilation of Tamils by Sri Lanka's Sinhalese-dominated government). Sometimes, new regimes can use the idea of cultural trauma to overcome their legitimation problems when they usurp power (notably communist regimes or the many instances of decolonisation in Africa where regime change is frequent). Sometimes, however, cultural trauma is successful in its persuasive meta-narrative and perpetrators have been compelled to accept moral responsibility (notably German acknowledgement of the Holocaust).

There is one complaint about the sociology of cultural trauma. The idea that the individual's personal experience of hurt and suffering ought to be the concern of ethics or psychology rather than sociology (Alexander 2012: 2) profoundly limits the sociological imagination, the key to which was, C. Wright Mills (1959b) argued, the intersection of personal biographical experience, social structure, power and history. What distinguishes the sociological approach developed in this chapter is its attention to individual personal experiences of trauma, rather than artful constructions of collective trauma to mediate group relations. I focus on what I call 'hidden victims' in order to bring personal biographical experience back into sociology's account of trauma. While my approach cannot explain all traumatic experiences, the framework draws on major sociological ideas, about silence, silencing, power, truth, inter-generational family relations, and moral obligations and duty, which connect individual biography, history, power and social structure within the sociological imagination. This represents, as I put it, notes towards a sociology of personal trauma.

Notes towards a sociology of personal trauma

Asking 'who is a victim' is one question. Asking who is *recognised* as a victim' is a significantly different question. The first addresses the person's lived experience of conflict-related harm, irrespective of whether it is real or imagined hurt, since imagined hurts are still felt as real; the second addresses the range of societal processes that influence the social construction of the victim category (on the social construction of the victim category, see Brewer et al. 2018: 26–34). One consequence of this social construction of the victim category is to neglect some victims, who become hidden, and thus subjected to processes of silencing, in which, through the operation of power, their voice is unheard. Silencing victims intensifies their suffering and trauma (see Schwab 2010; with respect to victims in Northern Rwanda, see Otake 2019). Social anthropologists show that silence can be cultural and in some contexts is expected (for example, Basso 1970). This is not the kind of silence that occurs in societies emerging out of conflict. Silence is beginning to enter into sociology, where Scott (2017, 2020), for example, links it to the 'sociology of nothingness' (passive omissions of not doing or not being; see also Murray and Durrheim 2021). Its application is more common in transitional justice (see, for example, Clark 2020; Eastmond and Selimovic 2014; Magadla 2021; Motsemme 2004; Selimovic 2018). The transitional justice literature places attention primarily on women's response to gendered violence and how their silence is a form of resistance or survival. Either as resistance or survival, silence represents a form of agency that communicates without words. The connection between silenced victims and hidden victims is very close, and I want to extend the reflections on silence by connecting silencing, hidden victims, inter-generational trauma and truth recovery that together point towards a sociological approach to personal trauma. The conceptual map of the sociology of personal trauma is represented in Figure 7.1.

All groups to a conflict have their preferred narrative and these narratives mostly compete. When what they say suits the narrative of one stakeholder or another, victims are canonised; when not, they are ignored, neglected and overlooked. All sides to a conflict have their 'preferred' and 'dis-preferred' victims and victim narratives; they are mostly different victims however, supporting and reinforcing contrary narratives. Who constitutes which kind of victim is entirely relative – and the same individual victim can be 'preferred' to one stakeholder and 'wrong' to another.

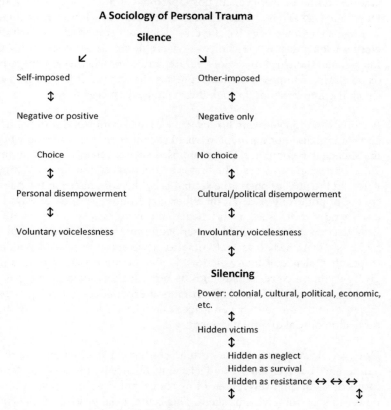

Figure 7.1   A sociology of personal trauma

Yet all parties to a conflict share in common the tendency to make certain victims saint-like and others unrecognised and hidden.

Canonisation paradoxically causes voicelessness for the majority of victims who are not saint-like. The voicelessness of the majority, however, can be 'self' or 'other' imposed. Self-imposed silence results from victims' withdrawal, repression, fear, anxiety, frustration, trauma and stress. This form of silence is not 'nothing' as Scott (2017, 2020) describes it in sociology; this silence does things and speaks of being. For example, some victims are silent deliberately so as not to traumatise their children and because they want to move on. This is silence by choice. In their study of silence amongst domestic labourers in post-apartheid South Africa, Murray and Durrheim (2021) refer to these as 'repressed silences'. However, we might distinguish between negative choices – where remembering is too painful emotionally; and positive choices – where decisions are taken to avoid inter-generational trauma. However, regardless of whether it is negative or positive self-imposed silence, repressed silences result in victims' personal disempowerment through their voluntary voicelessness.

Personal disempowerment, however, needs to be contrasted with political and cultural disempowerment in what I call other-imposed silence, where the silence is involuntary. Other-imposed silence reflects in involuntary voicelessness in two ways. The first is by the neglect of ordinary victims' voices in the public sphere; the second is by the dominance in the public sphere of politically partisan or rather lazy 'routine scripts' as ways for discussing victim issues in the media and in politics (see, for example, Brewer et al. 2018: 41–4). These scripts impute voice to victims but in highly standardised ways that come to represent cultural and political tropes that silence ordinary victims. Media attention that appears to be giving victims a voice actually ends up reproducing media stereotypes of victims, cultural caricatures of victimhood experiences, reducing victim issues to entertainment or newspaper sales. This is voicelessness by cultural and political disempowerment.

However, I want to make a further conceptual distinction. There is a difference between silence and silencing. Silence is voicelessness. Some forms of silence, however, are not by choice but from the application of power to keep some victims silent. This is the social process of silencing. Silencing involves the use of power to force involuntary silence. Silencing is an 'othering' process, to draw moral boundaries around excluded and marginal people and groups. Some women raped during the partition of India in 1947, for example, had their victimhood concealed within the family as a result of patriarchal power and the family's fear of social stigma (Butalia 2000). In post-genocide Rwanda, for example, the government's policies of institutionalising memorialisation of the genocide, prohibits talking about the genocide in public except in the 100 days reserved for official memorialisation. This institutionalised memory is really a form of institutionalised silencing (Brewer 2020). As Kelley (2017) argued, this manipulation of memory is a way of the regime maintaining power. Many women in Bosnia and Herzegovina are afraid to speak out about the sexual violence they suffered out of fear of reprisals from perpetrators (Selimovic 2018). In other words, silence actually speaks; it tells of absence, of what is disallowed and cannot be spoken. While silence in and of itself may not necessarily speak of powerlessness, since silence is a normal everyday practice in communication, *silencing* always speaks of power, fear and subjugation.

Silencing is a social process in which cultural, colonial, economic, political and patriarchal power is deployed to keep some victims involuntarily voiceless and silent. The process of silencing not only keeps those subjected to it voiceless; it keeps them hidden, without public recognition and without public acknowledgement. To forget a victim is to victimise them twice. Recognition and acknowledgement of their victimhood is important. Thus, involuntarily silenced victims experience a double victimhood. This double victimhood intensifies the traumatic hauntings they experience and keeps the ghosts alive.

Involuntarily silenced victims are what I call hidden victims and I suggest that the category of hidden victims needs to be isolated and interrogated to identify its special features. Who do I have in mind to illustrate the category? A number come to mind as examples, not all of whom we think of as victims whenever the category is socially constructed:

- Women subjected to gender-based sexual violence and rape in war (see, for example, Hynes 2004; Littlewood 1997);
- Men and boys subjected to male rape in war (see, for example, Clark 2017; Weiss 2010);
- Children born of rape during war (for Rwanda, see Torgovnik 2009);
- There are hidden victims of collusion and state crimes, particularly where the state regime survived (for Northern Ireland, see Cadwallader 2013; Punch 2012; Unwin 2016);
- Informers and collaborators of failed regimes, such as the so-called 'disappeared' in Argentina and Northern Ireland, and what in South Africa are called the *askari* (on Cyprus and Spain, see Kovras 2013);
- State veterans, especially those from defeated regimes or who were forced to become perpetrators (on Afrikaans conscripts, see Verwoerd and Edlmann 2021); and

110 ADVANCED INTRODUCTION TO THE SOCIOLOGY OF PEACE PROCESSES

- Ex-combatants, particularly amongst non-state actors where there has been no regime change (see the many cases in Brewer and Wahidin 2021).

These examples illustrate that they are hidden for a number of different reasons and hidden from a number of different sorts of people. First, for example, hidden victims are largely found amongst the vanquished, the defeated side in war; this is true of state veterans on the losing side, as well as defeated non-state ex-combatants. A victor's peace, such as in Sri Lanka, where one side wins militarily and the other is vanquished, tends to neglect victims in the defeated group, silencing them, as happens to Sri Lanka's defeated Tamils. Some states that survive focus solely on the 'preferred' victims from their own side.

Second, states that emerge out of conflict can sometimes lack the economic and infrastructural capacity to develop victim policies and to promote victims' voices; or they do so only temporarily in the immediate aftermath of conflict, thereafter removing victims from the mainstream of public policy and political attention. There is a sense of incompleteness amongst many victims of apartheid in South Africa who feel society has moved on beyond them. This feeling is also present amongst some *Umkhonto we Sizwe* veterans, who formed the armed wing of the African National Congress, who feel ignored by the ANC government (see Langa, Maringira and Merafe 2021).

Third, defeated states leave a legacy for their state veterans that tends to ignore their claims to victimhood. In South Africa, for example, there is need to recognise that Black police in the old South African Police (on which, see Brewer 1994) mostly became agents of apartheid out of poverty. This applies also to young Afrikaans- and English-speakers as conscripts who had little voluntarism when legally obliged to defend the indefensible (see Verwoerd and Edlmann 2021). These sorts of perpetrator are what Loyle and Davenport (2020), from their Rwandan study, refer to as 'murderers in the middle', forced to kill by orders from above (which Elster 2004 argues is one of the mitigations 'wrong-doers' make). And ex-combatants' moral claims to victimhood are especially contested where the regime they fought against survives or their use of violence remains contested, at least outside their support base, such as members of the Revolutionary Armed Forces of Colombia–People's Army (see Mun et al. 2021) and the IRA in Northern Ireland (on the moral claims to legitimacy made by paramilitary members in Northern Ireland, see Brewer 2021a).

Fourth, members of dominant and powerful groups, who get to define history, to define the preferred narrative of the war, can shape the politics of memory in such a way as to ignore some victims. This is a kind of denial of the past – and thus a denial of some people's victimhood. The past is viewed with a subjective lens that ignores the victimhood of some groups – only in recent years, for example, have the British come to recognise the victimhood of ordinary Germans caught up in the Second World War and its immediate aftermath. The victimhood of Irish Catholics who fought in the military in service for the colonial power of the British Crown is not fully recognised, especially by Ulster Protestants who want to keep military sacrifice as their special reason for Union with Britain and as a mark of their Britishness.

Finally, cultural and political processes that create a hierarchy of victimhood also create hidden victims, those at the bottom of the hierarchy whose claim to victimhood is contested. This particularly affects perpetrators, which is a category that is socially constructed in ways opposite to that of victim. Note here, for example, the difficulties Republic and Loyalist ex-combatants have in Northern Ireland with being classed as victims (Brewer 2021a). Subordinate groups in conflict with the powerful operate a reverse principle, in which they fail to see that state veterans can be victims too, even if they are victims in a different way. The moral claims to victimhood by state veterans are rarely acknowledged. Veterans from Britain's recent counter-insurgency wars in Afghanistan, for example, are not usually thought of as victims (see, for example, Brewer and Herron 2021).

Power, in other words, is deployed in a process of silencing to intentionally strip the voice from some victims. Power, we know sociologically, is of many types, and they overlap. Colonisation, for example, was often used to enforce sexual exploitation and violence against indigenous women (see, for example, Coetzee and Du Toit 2018); sexualisation and racialisation of indigenous peoples was a key aspect of colonialism. Sexualised and racialised indigenous peoples epitomise the category of hidden victims.

112 ADVANCED INTRODUCTION TO THE SOCIOLOGY OF PEACE PROCESSES

However, the power to impose involuntary silence is of many kinds, and can be:

- Cultural power (such as by imposing feelings of shame, stigma, ethno-religious sensitivities about shame, etc.);
- Colonial and post-colonial power (such as by neglecting the appropriated and dispossessed 'other');
- Political power (such as wars of decolonisation, and the repression of the victimhood experiences of the vanquished, defeated and powerless);
- Economic power (such as the repression of the voice of the poor); and
- Patriarchal power (such as the silencing of women, children, and those subjected to sexual and gender-based violence, and domestic violence).

In other words, the biographical experience of silencing as a social process, which is referred to here as enforced and involuntary silence, intersects with history, such as in the form of colonial dispossession and past wars of decolonisation, and with power in all the forms described above. Social structural conditions develop from this intersection of history and power – stratification hierarchies, differentiation in the social statuses of people, racial, colonial and ethnic divisions, and the like – to create social conditions that encourage and impose silencing as a social process. The intersectionality of race, gender, class and colonialism isolates and disadvantages particular categories of person – colonised, Black, poor women and children, for example – that turns them into silenced 'hidden victims'.

If I can extend the conceptualisation of hidden victims a little more, it is important to isolate three measures of hiddenness for those victims who are involuntarily silenced: hiddenness as neglect; hiddenness as survival; and hiddenness as resistance. Hiddenness as neglect is obvious. Many kinds of victims are hidden by sheer neglect of them. We must distinguish neglect from hiddenness as a survival strategy. Keeping quiet to survive is not a positive choice; it is a means of survival against the very power processes that create fear to raise one's voice. It is represented well by the quiescence that many colonised groups develop out of fear of oppression from the colonising power; this is the kind of quiescence we saw in Black politics in South Africa between the 1961 Sharpeville massacre and the 1976 Soweto uprising (on which, see Brewer 1986b). Quiescence is adopted by many victims of gendered and sexual violence as a survival

NOTES TOWARDS A SOCIOLOGY OF PERSONAL TRAUMA   113

strategy, who are reluctant to give themselves a voice because of male dominance. Domestic violence is also often shrouded in silence by its victims.

This brings us neatly to hiddenness as resistance and the way hiddenness can be transcended in acts of resistance against the social process of silencing. There are many acts of resistance, some of which include:

- self-mobilisation to develop the confidence and courage to speak (to disclose formerly secret information);
- public telling of hidden narratives (using opportunities in public space, in civil society or in politics, to narrate the forgotten victimhood story);
- initiating third-party advocacy (such as done on behalf of Palestinians by Arab governments and many Western human rights groups);
- the use of litigation in criminal courts to disclose crimes (in local and international criminal courts);
- utilising diaspora networks to disclose formerly concealed information (such as done by Tamils exiled across the world and by Irish-American Catholics in the USA); and
- promoting political change, including regime change that rewards inclusivity of narratives (such as promoted by the Black Consciousness Movement in apartheid South Africa).

I have a final observation on the category of hidden victims. If neglect is primarily passive, hiddenness as survival and as resistance involves agency. Even the strategy of keeping silent as survival – a kind of strategic muteness – involves social action by deliberative agents. Agency is even more evident in resistance. Agency in the form of resistance brings me to the most important theme in the sociology of personal trauma.

Hidden victims struggle over their identity, a struggle over how to find out the truth behind their victimhood. And when hiddenness is resisted, there is the struggle over winning recognition and acknowledgement. These struggles have the paradoxical effect of *increasing* their anger and intensifying their feelings of shame and guilt, perpetuating the traumatic ghosts, and inhibiting the process of reconciliation and healing in society. Fundamentally, it increases the likelihood of inter-generational trauma as children and grandchildren are turned into 'guardians of the past' to ensure the truth comes out about their loved one's victimhood. Children and grandchildren of hidden victims tend to inherit a family

114 ADVANCED INTRODUCTION TO THE SOCIOLOGY OF PEACE PROCESSES

responsibility to keep the past alive for their relatives' sake. Disclosure of the truth becomes a moral duty, a moral obligation passed down the generations, reproducing the hauntings from the past. I want to emphasise the significance of this. Hiddenness as resistance is transformed ethically into the moral duty in subsequent generations to disclose the truth; and where truth is denied, inter-generational trauma is transmitted down the generations.

Collusion and the moral duty to truth in Northern Ireland

I want to take a detour in this argument for a moment to demonstrate from real-life victims of collusion in Northern Ireland that this ethical duty is truly born down the generations. Victims of collusion epitomise 'hidden' and silenced victims, which is why they have been selected here from amongst the many different kinds of victims 'the Troubles' tragically created. The data comes from the MA dissertation of one of my students whom I had the privilege to supervise, Elizabeth Carberry (2019), whose father, Stan Carberry, was himself killed in suspicious circumstances by British soldiers in the early 1970s when she was five years old and who still awaits information about his death, let alone justice and closure. She interviewed a small sample of women all of whom had close family members killed by the British security forces in disputed circumstances or by Loyalist paramilitaries suspected of working in collusion with the security forces. One of the women had a close family member killed in Bloody Sunday, January 1972, another in the Ballymurphy Massacre, August 1971, when British army troops opened with live fire on civil rights marchers and bystanders alike, killing, amongst others, children, a priest, and a mother of eight. Official legal enquiries into both events have now disclosed, up to fifty years later, that those murdered were entirely innocent of the claims made by the security forces and the British government at the time that they were engaged in violence.

The dissertation captures well the sample's anger, frustration and disillusion. 'It left me feeling angry, frustrated and … angry at the British army and angry about what happened him' (quoted in Carberry 2019: 45); 'my husband he thinks we will never get truth, they never admit to nothing … you would like them to be able to admit to doing it' (2019: 46); 'I'm angry with probably the higher up level, angry with the British government that they allowed collusion, you know it was one of their strategies and that's what I'm angry with' (2019: 46). This anger, they are aware, has passed

NOTES TOWARDS A SOCIOLOGY OF PERSONAL TRAUMA 115

down the generations. A mother reflected on the impact that the death of her parent has had on her own children and is worth quoting at length:

> I'm ruining my kids' lives because I won't let them out of my sight, and I don't know how to change ... I know I did damage to my own two girls I know that for a fact I see it now ... the damage that I did [sad expression]. I think if I had of had help sooner proper help sooner, then my girls wouldn't be as affected today as they are. I had a fear that somebody was gonna try and throw acid at her, somebody was gonna steal her, was gonna try and hurt her ... I just had this fear that I wasn't gonna live to see them grow up that something was gonna happen. Like everybody else, we were tortured. The Brits kicked in the door in the middle of the night threatened to arrest my daddy and hit my daddy, had us on the sofas squealing and crying from all hours ... I knew [her close family member] was shot but I didn't know, none of us knew the whole extent of it. (quoted in Carberry 2019: 47)

'I mean', one tragically said, 'I've damaged my kids. My heart breaks because it's like looking at me' (quoted in Carberry 2019: 56).

They have not lost their moral sensitivity, however. This sensitivity made some aware that soldiers, some of whom they confront in enquiries or court rooms, must now be feeling the same trauma they do, although this does not assuage their own traumatic hauntings. As one respondent remarked: 'Oh these soldiers are in there, oh my god they're old men and they're in ill health and they've PSTD [sic] or whatever the hell you call it. And I'm sitting there going, I have that, I have that, I get that, I take antidepressants, I'm getting trauma counselling, I self-harm' (quoted in Carberry 2019: 48).

The key point, however, is that subsequent generations feel the obligation to continue the search for truth and justice. Passing the obligation down the generations to overcome hiddenness, to gain recognition, acknowledgement and truth, made one woman reflect on how, now, younger faces are appearing in courts, tribunals and enquiries where the truth is sought: 'You can see more young faces at the court and at the meetings needing to know what's going on you know, it used to be, it used to be elderly people' (quoted in Carberry 2019: 55). One woman said about the obligation she felt to her father, whose own father – her grandfather – was killed, 'aw daddy, I'm doing this for you' (quoted in Carberry 2019: 53). Another is

116 ADVANCED INTRODUCTION TO THE SOCIOLOGY OF PEACE PROCESSES

worth quoting at length and actually uses the word 'duty' when describing her motivation:

> With regards [to] the drive and what motivates me as [name of close family member deleted] sister, probably because my mum has stopped, and I think it's like this duty that I feel that somebody has to continue on to try and fight for some justice. You know the truth has to come out some road along down the line ... It has to ... I think my family deserver [sic] it I think every family that's lost loved ones deserve it you know in fairness, I really do. Some say the truth will seep out no matter how much you try to hide it, it does seep out over time. It's just unfortunate that it takes so long. (quoted in Carberry 2019: 54)

Referring to the death of her father and the laying down of the burden to find the truth to her son, one respondent said: 'I feel, do you see if it were me, daddy would have left no stone unturned. He would have got to the bottom of it and now I owe that to him. See if anything happens [to me], I always say to [name of son], see if anything happens to me, will you make sure that someone, you carry it on for me. I'd like somebody to see it to the end' (quoted in Carberry 2019: 57). Some respondents thus reflected on how their children had taken up the fight for justice. Referring to her daughter, one said: 'she has taken over now nearly where I'm leaving off because I am not fit anymore ... oh, it's very important to have ... we are fighting for the last 28 years' (quoted in Carberry 2019: 57). The ghosts are enduring, as one said: 'I'm not going to give up and I will continue to seek some sort of justice ... and I won't give up and if I happen to pass [die] I will make sure that my children pursue this as long as it takes, and you know what they always put in the delaying mechanisms at all times but I don't care if it's a hundred years down the line' (quoted in Carberry 2019: 57).

In short, the moral obligation, the duty, is passed down the generations, along with the trauma: 'I feel a duty, a real duty to my grandad to keep on going' (quoted in Carberry 2019: 58). People are socialised into moral duties, not taught them or have them forced upon them, 'it's in you' as one said: 'a duty, a duty of something, I don't know if you would call it a duty, but it's ... it is passed down, it's not asked you know, it's not asked of anybody you know, it's in you, you know' (quoted in Carberry 2019: 58). Unspoken family obligations, in other words, become obligations down the generations to discover the truth.

Moral duty, untruth and personal trauma

There is a paradox for hidden victims that gets to the crux of the sociology of their personal trauma. It is power imbalances that cause some victims to be hidden in the first place and these same power inequalities can keep them hidden, perpetuating the hauntings. Inter-generational trauma thus becomes almost inherent in hidden victims. Therefore, second- and third-generation victims imbued with a moral duty to resist hiddenness are fated to reproduce the ghosts when they have no control over the truth recovery process. The deployment of power to reproduce hiddenness and maintain involuntary silence makes it extremely difficult for the next generations to disclose the truth to fulfil their moral duty. Inter-generational trauma for this category of victim is thus in direct correlation with the control powerful groups and institutions have over the disclosure of truth.

In particular, state regimes that remain intact after violence try to limit access to truth. For political reasons they seek to limit disclosure of their human rights abuses, collusion and other state crimes, whether perpetrated by state forces directly or by state-affiliated and co-opted paramilitaries. Changes in state regimes facilitate greater disclosure as part of post-conflict truth recovery processes. Even here, however, the disclosure can be constrained by the new regime, such as in Sri Lanka with the fall of the Rajapaksa regime. Disclosure is also affected by the simple practical limits imposed on truth recovery procedures; which was the case, for example, in the South African Truth and Reconciliation Commission (see especially Motsemme 2004; Wilson 2001). Even long-established democratic states try to limit knowledge of their engagement in dirty wars, as occurs in Northern Ireland with respect to the British state's collusion with paramilitaries and with the crimes of its soldiers (see Cadwallader 2013; Punch 2012; Unwin 2016). States, however, are not the only ones in control of information that can enable subsequent generations to meet their moral obligations to truth on behalf of their hidden victim relatives. Knowledge of the whereabouts of the disappeared, knowledge about the circumstances around killings and bombings by paramilitary groups, and knowledge of the identity of rapists responsible for gendered and sexual violence, are examples of the lack of information that keeps some victims hidden.

However, a powerful lesson of history is that repressed memories have a tendency to resurface sometime later when circumstances change to make them visible, speakable and listenable. Memory holes exist in the past and they are filled with ghosts that haunt hidden victims' present and their future. Hidden victims who resist and who wish to fill these memory holes have a kind of 'shouting silence'; a silence that speaks, rages, against all those who control access to the truth. Resistance to hiddenness, despite it being turned ethical, becomes a struggle against those who control truth recovery. My argument is that slaying ghosts for hidden victims develops at the pace of truth; untruth keeps the traumatic ghosts alive.

Conclusion

The personal trauma of hidden victims and their children and grandchildren is deeply sociological. This is not to refute the importance of psychology, psychotherapy and psychoanalysis for helping hurting people, or the relevance of cultural trauma in understanding the painful social memory of groups, but sociology can also help us understand how the personal trauma of hidden victims is reproduced within the family and across the generations. As I have shown in this chapter, the category of hidden victim is itself profoundly sociological, reflecting the intersection of biographical experience, social structure, history and power that is able to explain the process of silencing that enforces involuntary silence on some victims, and especially on hidden victims. The transmission of personal trauma is also sociological, reflecting family processes that obligate subsequent generations to fulfil what is a moral duty to disclose the truth about their relatives' victimhood; and the power of some to withhold this truth transmits inter-generational trauma. Personal trauma is thus at the centre of several key sociological processes. These include power, and its various forms; history, especially of colonialism and imperial power; biographical experience, especially of violence in its many forms, including gendered violence; and social structure, including the intersection of 'race', class, stratification hierarchies and colonialism. These are processes that C. Wright Mills said were at the heart of the promise of the sociological imagination, and I cannot demur from this view.

8 Conclusion: why the sociology of peace processes matters

Introduction

I have had the privilege of supervising over fifty students to successful submission of their PhD and I have told every one of them that their conclusion should be short and be in two parts. The first, normally constituting about one third of the length, should summarise the argument; the second, which is the most important part of the whole thesis, should answer the 'so what?' question: why is it important that the reader knows this? What is its wider significance? I intend here to follow my own advice.

Summary of the argument

I began at the beginning. It was necessary to commence at the very foundation of the discipline of sociology to highlight its neglect of peace as a topic, which required a return to a hoary old debate from the past about order and conflict. Neither the sociologies of order or conflict problematised peace as a sociological process, despite peace being connected to the systems and processes that reproduce order and which restore it when conflict breaks it down. However, I emphasised that the sociologies of order and conflict are not two different paradigms but two sides of the same Janus face, with consensus and change being one social process. Moral cohesion, the typical concern of the sociology of order, presupposes order and competition, cohesiveness and conflict. Moral cohesion cannot exist without distributive fairness, social justice, equality

119

of opportunity and compromise. And it is this, after all, that sustains the discipline's interest in war and violence, which has vastly surpassed that in peace. However, the sociology of war implicates the sociology of peace and peace processes, since war and peace are also indivisible. Indeed, sociologists of violence and war have themselves identified the grounds on which changes to the practice of war in late modernity, called 'new wars', necessitate a new focus on peace. Peace, in other words, is now on sociology's agenda.

Peace has now been recognised as deeply sociological as a result of what I called 'the political economy of re-enchantment' within late modernity. Two claims are embedded here. The first is that the social sciences have experienced a second cognitivist revolution in which interest has been awakened in affective and emotional issues such as love, anger, suffering, hate, revenge, tolerance, compromise, vulnerability, human dignity and the like, that represent a re-enchantment of their subject matter. The sociological literature on these themes is considerable and doyens of the discipline are engaging with them. The second claim is that we should locate this re-enchantment within a political economy. Five features distinguish the structural and material conditions that mark the political economy of re-enchantment: a violent hegemonic globalisation that simultaneously involves the globalisation of peace; the intensification of wealth inequalities and disparities, between the Global North and Global South but also within the Global North amongst people left behind by neo-liberal capitalism; new forms of war that have deepened the moral degradations of violence; the collapse of the public–private distinction, which has domesticated the public sphere and made formerly private emotions public; and the disjuncture between the growth of moral responsibility to distant strangers and the hostility to them when they appear in our midst, which leads to a process of 'othering' and intensifies feelings of fear and threat towards those considered different.

The political economy of re-enchantment creates an intellectual space for the sociology of peace processes alongside those other themes that reflect the second cognitivist revolution in social science. A new approach was outlined through which we understood peace sociologically, drawing a contrast between five antinomies, which enrich what we mean by peace. 'Reconciliation' is so in vogue in the study of peace processes amongst academics (see Kelly 2021), practitioners and lay people, but it is a rather vacuous and empty term to describe peace, despite its moral and ethical

CONCLUSION: WHY THE SOCIOLOGY OF PEACE PROCESSES MATTERS 121

connotations. A sociological definition of peace infills the term reconciliation, broadening it to include active (rather than passive) peace, positive (rather than negative) peace, social transformation (not just conflict transformation), peacebuilding (as well as statebuilding), and the social peace process (not just the political peace process). The effect of this enrichment is that sociology sees peace as the restoration of social solidarity after conflict, which is itself dependent on the restoration of sociability. This sense of social togetherness requires the restoration of sociability, of living together in tolerance despite difference. Social solidarity and sociability are mediated, however, by social justice. Continued social *in*justice stymies the restoration of sociability amongst erstwhile enemies and inhibits the development of senses of social solidarity. As I argued, this alliteration of solidarity, sociability and social justice requires us to rethink what we mean by peace; peace without social justice is not peace at all.

To flesh out what we mean sociologically by a peace process, I used three axes, relational distance–closeness, spatial separation–territorial integrity, and cultural capital–cultural annihilation, to identify three types of peace process, which I called conquest (via a victor's peace), cartography (with peace via partition), and compromise (with peace via a mutually agreed second preference settlement). The connections between these axes were plotted in Figure 3.1, which helps sociology isolate the importance of the third type, compromise peace processes, which, while the most ethically appropriate is also the most difficult, requiring an approach to peace based on sociology's broader and fuller understanding of it. 'Reconciliation' does not come near to capturing the scale of the problems compromise peace processes face, or their solutions. Sociology facilitates a post-reconciliation approach to compromise peace processes.

I suggested that the sociological definition of peace and the associated typology of peace processes offer a new empirical research agenda for the study of compromise peace processes. This is not a comprehensive list of issues in compromise peace processes to which sociology could contribute, but compromise peace processes, for example, throw up a range of problems which sociology can help understand. These range from the social construction of victimhood that creates a reprehensible victim hierarchy; the moral confusion around the ex-combatant or perpetrator category and their own claims to legitimacy; the social construction of ex-combatants as martyrs, heroes or demons; the deconstruction of

122 ADVANCED INTRODUCTION TO THE SOCIOLOGY OF PEACE PROCESSES

violent masculinities; women's fight for gender equality; legacy issues revolving around truth, memory and dealing with the past; as well an array of post-conflict emotions from forgiveness to rage, hate to love, and anger to mercy.

Part of the programmatic outline of the sociology of peace processes thus involved offering a sociological account of new concepts that emerge for the discipline once we address the sociology of peace process. Several chapters were devoted to developing concepts like the sociology of compromise; the sociologies of post-conflict emotions, such as anger, forgiveness, mercy, hope and social trust; the sociology of everyday life peacebuilding; and the sociology of personal trauma. The thrust of these chapters was threefold: to show what the discipline of sociology can offer to illuminate such concepts; to identify the insights mainstream sociologists could offer to the analysis of peace processes if they paid them attention; and what specialists from other disciplines can learn, theoretically and empirically, from the sociology of peace processes.

So what?

The weight of this argument is that it isolates the importance of moral sensibility both to sociology as a discipline and to the analysis of compromise peace processes. This book, in other words, is part of its own subject matter by itself reflecting the re-enchantment of social science.

The sociology of peace processes as I have laid it out its prospectus, obligates sociology to address the social processes that form and restore moral sensibility after conflict, while also obligating society to take back control and ownership of peace processes from politicians, whose adversarial discourse is inimical to dealing with the restoration of moral sensibility.

Moral sensibility and sociology

This book has been much more than a programmatic outline of a new area of study within sociology, although there is this; it has argued that the sociology of peace processes implicates a new kind of sociology. I have argued for this new way of doing sociology in the past, when I referred to the new public value social science (Brewer 2013a) that made sociologists'

CONCLUSION: WHY THE SOCIOLOGY OF PEACE PROCESSES MATTERS 123

moral commitments and value orientations legitimate inasmuch as they served what I called the normative public value of social science. I defined this normative public value as follows:

> The normative public value of social science is that it nurtures a moral sentiment in which we produce and reproduce the social nature of society, enabling us to recognise each other as social beings with a shared responsibility for the future of humankind through understanding, explaining, analysing and ameliorating the fundamental social problems stored up for us. Social science thus becomes a public good for its own sake for cultivating this moral sentiment and sympathetic imagination through its subject matter, teaching, research and civic engagements. (2013a: 151)

I extended this later (Brewer 2014b) by arguing that sociologists need to make society their vocation as a way of ethically renewing their practice.

Sociology has normative public value, therefore, by making people aware of themselves as comprising a society, helping in the development and dissemination of key social values that make society possible – social sensibilities like trust, empathy, altruism, tolerance, compromise, compassion, social solidarity and senses of belonging – and assisting in society's ongoing betterment and improvement and the elimination of social suffering and harm (Brewer 2013a: 151). This is sociologists' vocation to society: the social renewal of society in order to realise moral sensibility and social justice (Brewer 2014b). This permits sociologists to escape cultural relativism in order to make legitimate moral claims, identifying some things as objectively wrong in that they promote social suffering and harm and do not promote social betterment and improvement. Sociologists' moral responsibilities can be discussed amongst ourselves and the public in open dialogue, as debate about the idea of public sociology or public social science does, but by no moral standard is female genital mutilation acceptable; no set of cultural values can see good or right in migrants' babies being washed up on seashores drowned in vain attempts to seek protection. It is objectively evil to morally enervate your enemy that you defile and degrade their bodies, cutting foetuses from women's wombs, or engaging in genocidal mass murder. I will not go on amplifying the horrors for my point is clear. Not only does this normative public value encompass new sorts of topics and subject matter in sociology; it implicates a new way of approaching sociology by giving it an ethical purpose.

Sociology, in short, has moral sensibility as its domain. This central socio-logical concern with moral sentiment, as I have said before (Brewer 2013a: 156, 2014a) returns the discipline to where I at least locate its strong-est origins in Britain, the Scottish moralists of the eighteenth-century Scottish Enlightenment, as I argued in Chapter 2. And like the Scottish moralists, sociologists who are committed to the normative public value of the discipline are able to make moral claims, to argue for the good society and against social conditions that threaten it. Sociology has an ethical purpose. In the case of peace processes this value commitment is to emancipate society from violence and to turn the objective of a shared future into a moral duty.

This was the backcloth to my programmatic outline of the sociology of peace processes that made moral sensibility its central motif. Peace emerges as a sociological issue out of a moral reawakening in the social sciences at the end of the twentieth century. This is far greater than the moral backlash to the degradations and humiliations of late modernity's 'new wars'; it reflects a wider re-enchantment that has material and structural causes but with profound affective, emotional and moral outworkings in the discipline. I thus made moral sensibility central to my sociological definition of peace, as well as to the triad of sociability, social solidarity and social justice that marks the success of a compromise peace process. Moral sensibility shapes the attention of the sociology of peace processes away from the past towards the future and is the central concern behind the responsibility model of a shared society in the future. The moral concerns of the sociology of peace processes are thus entirely consistent with the moral turn in sociology as a discipline.

Moral sensibility and the limits of politics

Dealing now with the significance of moral sensibility to peace processes, it is necessary to distinguish three levels through which moral sensibility mediates the success of compromise peace processes: by representing the problems facing compromise peace processes as moral ones as much as political; by its attention to the critical role of society over politics; and by its attention to the future, not the past.

Peace processes are too important to be left to politicians (see Brewer 2021b for elaboration). Political discourse is confrontational and adver-sarial, not suited to dealing with complex moral issues. Above all, political

CONCLUSION: WHY THE SOCIOLOGY OF PEACE PROCESSES MATTERS 125

discourse is past- and present-focused, to use my characterisation of post-conflict emotions, not forward-focused. Politicians' sense of the future extends only to the next election; they do not have the same interest I have in what the future will be like for my grandchildren. Their value orientation towards and vision of the future is only what they think will win them the next election. The deeply complex moral issues affecting compromise peace processes identified by the sociology of peace processes are better addressed outside the chambers and institutions which reproduce this kind of political discourse.

That is to say, society is the space for discussing the moral ambiguities and complexities of learning to live together in tolerance after conflict. I have argued many times before that this includes key social spaces like civil society (Brewer 2010), sacred social spaces, including religion (Brewer, Higgins and Teeney 2011), and everyday life spaces (Brewer et al. 2018), affecting women's groups, young people, business, the trade unions, universities, NGOs, church groups and the like.

When peace is understood sociologically as the trinity of sociability, social solidarity and social justice, moral sensibility mediates the success of peace processes, not politicians. Moral sensibility is measured by regard for the human dignity of erstwhile enemies, by respect for diversity and difference, readiness to accept that rights bring duties, including the duty to accept that others also have rights, and by emotional empathy to others, what I referred to in Chapter 4 as the intersubjective relational ethic of 'getting along' that is the basis of sociability and for the reproduction of society itself after conflict. This relational ethic highlights the critical importance of studying the emotional landscape of people in compromise peace processes, for the emotional interiority of people learning to live together in moral sensibility after conflict is the key to the success of compromise peace processes. This makes it important to open up discussion of the array of cognitive issues vital to the restoration of moral sensibility and social solidarity, and thus to the success of compromise peace processes. As I have argued, these cognitive issues include anger, forgiveness, mercy, forgetting, hope, trust and memory, amongst others. However, I showed that the social practice of compromise that makes moral sensibility possible, works under the constraints and opportunities of social structure, personal biography and history, and its potential is affected by compromise mediators that press heavily upon it. Moral sensibility, thus, can quickly disappear if social transformation is absent and social injustices remain.

While the success of compromise peace processes is bedevilled by legacy issues that essentially involve refighting the morality of the past, whether the conflict and its suffering were morally legitimate and worth it, compromise peace processes should be more concerned with the future than the past. Legacy lasts a lifetime, of course, in victims' damaged bodies and minds, but the future is generations long. In Chapter 3, however, I discussed the problems around pathological memory cultures and the ways in which they burden the future by obsession with the past (for greater detail, see Brewer 2020, 2021b). To highlight the importance of moral issues to considerations of the future, I want to sociologically deconstruct what it means to share. This isolates the importance of moral sensibility, which again takes us well beyond politicians' rhetoric of 'shared societies' by treating sharing as a moral issue.

As I have discussed elsewhere (Brewer 2021b), in one sense when we share, we divide up, apportion and allocate: sometimes equally, but mostly unequally. Sharing determines how access to a joint resource, good or space is distributed. I call this the *distribution model of sharing*; it divvies up and allots. It is essentially amoral for the allocation is done regardless of the moral purpose of sharing as a form of social interaction. It is the kind of sharing done on economic markets. This is why equality in the size of the shares is irrelevant in the distribution model. Sharing, in this meaning of the term, is instrumental not moral; it is merely a distribution mechanism. What matters is that proportions are distributed, regardless of their equality.

In another sense, however, sharing means to participate in, to use, enjoy, or experience a resource, good or space jointly. In this view, we hold the resource, good or space together with others, having a share of the responsibility for it. Again, this is not necessarily equal responsibility, but it nonetheless requires shared commitments. I call this the *responsibility model of sharing*. It determines that a resource, good or space we jointly enjoy and experience, is the responsibility of everyone who shares it. With responsibility comes moral obligation; it is not just instrumental. Where we share a resource, good or space with someone and have responsibility in common towards it, sharing imposes a moral obligation to ensure that whatever it is that is experienced, enjoyed or participated in together

CONCLUSION: WHY THE SOCIOLOGY OF PEACE PROCESSES MATTERS 127

remains shared and joint. In the responsibility model, the moral obligation is to ensure the resource, good or space remains jointly shared. It is the responsibility towards it that remains common; it does not have to be experienced in a common way.

Applying these models to the idea of a shared future in compromise peace processes, the responsibility model suggests that a shared future does not mean that everybody must develop a rainbow identity, as Mandela once put it for post-apartheid South Africa. It is not about garnering a future that is exactly the same for everyone who inherits it. A shared future means having a common responsibility for its delivery and maintenance and feeling a moral obligation to ensure the future is jointly experienced, enjoyed and participated in regardless of differences. The distribution model of sharing delivers difference; it does so by allocating and dividing up differentially. The responsibility model manages difference by transcending it under the moral obligation to share.

This affirms some of the central arguments advanced in this book that the problem compromise peace processes face in achieving a shared future is not so much political but moral. The responsibility model of a shared future is inherently moral because there is an obligation on every individual who desires a shared society to help achieve it. It is not just the responsibility of politicians, nor even of civil society; it is society's responsibility as a whole. A shared future is a moral not a political idea and people's responsibility to ensure the future is shared constitutes itself as a moral duty, not a political goal. Under the moral obligation to jointly share the future, which is the overriding principle of the responsibility model, those committed to sharing cannot consider their own identity, and its social, cultural and political expressions, as the only identity relevant to the future. Sharing responsibility for the future requires toleration of difference and thus the move away from zero-sum notions of identity. Commitment to the moral obligations of the responsibility model perforce implies the end of zero-sum identities. Learning to live together is then understood as a moral duty; it is about garnering moral sensibility, not realising instrumental ends. Let this be the signal conclusion to the sociology of peace processes.

References

Abell, P. (1991) 'Homo Sociologicus: Do We Need Him/Her?', *Sociological Theory* 9(2): 195–8.

Adam, H. and Moodley, K. (2015) *Imagined Liberation*. Philadelphia: Temple University Press.

Adler, P.A., Adler, P. and Fontana, A. (1987) 'Everyday Life Sociology', *Annual Review of Sociology* 13: 217–35.

Akenson, D. (1992) *God's People*. London: Cornell University Press.

Alexander, J. (2004) 'Toward a Theory of Cultural Trauma' in J. Alexander, R. Eyerman, B. Giesen, N. Smelser and P. Sztompka, *Cultural Trauma and Collective Identity*. Berkeley: University of California Press: 1–30.

Alexander, J. (2012) *Trauma: A Social Theory*. Cambridge: Polity Press.

Alexander, J., Eyerman, R., Giesen, B., Smelser, N. and Sztompka, P. (2004) *Cultural Trauma and Collective Identity*. Berkeley: University of California Press.

Archard, D. (2012) 'Moral Compromise', *Philosophy* 87(3): 403–20.

Archer, M. (2000a) 'Homo Economicus, Homo Sociologicus and Homo Sentiens', in M. Archer and J. Tritter (eds), *Rational Choice Theory*. London: Routledge: 36–56.

Archer, M. (2000b) *Being Human*. Cambridge: Cambridge University Press.

Arendt, H. (1958) *The Human Condition*. Chicago: University of Chicago Press.

Atack, I. (2005) *The Ethics of Peace and War*. Edinburgh: Edinburgh University Press.

Bailey, J. (2000) 'Some Meanings of "The Private" in Sociological Thought', *Sociology* 34: 381–401.

Bandura, A. (1989) 'Human Agency in Social Cognitive Theory', *American Psychologist* 44: 1175–84.

Bar-Tal, D. (2001) 'Why Does Fear Override Hope in Societies Engulfed by Intractable Conflict, As It Does in the Israeli Society?', *Political Psychology* 22: 601–27.

Basso, S. (1970) '"To Give Up on Words": Silence in Western Apache Culture', *Journal of Anthropological Research* 26(3): 213–50.

Bauman, Z. (1991) *Modernity and the Holocaust*. Cambridge: Polity Press.

Bauman, Z. (1998) *Globalisation: The Human Consequences*. Cambridge: Polity Press.

Baume, S. and Novak, S. (eds) (2020) *Compromises in Democracy*. London: Palgrave.

REFERENCES 129

Beck, U. (1992) *The Risk Society*. London: Sage.

Beck, U. (1999) *The World Risk Society*. Cambridge: Polity Press.

Beck, U. (2010) *A God of One's Own*. Cambridge: Polity Press.

Bendix, R. (1966) *Max Weber*. London: Methuen.

Bennett, T. and Watson, D. (eds) (2002) *Understanding Everyday Life*. Oxford: Blackwell.

Benton, T. (1978) 'How Many Sociologies?', *The Sociological Review* 26(2): 217–36.

Berliner, D. (2005) 'The Abuses of Memory', *Anthropological Quarterly* 78(1): 197–211.

Blustein, J. (2014) *Forgiveness and Remembrance*. Oxford: Oxford University Press.

Boltanski, L. (1999) *Distant Suffering*. Cambridge: Cambridge University Press.

Boudon, R. (2006) '*Homo Sociologicus:* Neither a Rational or an Irrational Idiot', *Papers* 80: 149–69.

Braithwaite, J. (2020) *Restorative Justice and Responsive Regulation*. Oxford: Oxford University Press.

Braithwaite, J. and Mugford, S. (1994) 'Conditions of Successful Reintegration Ceremonies', *British Journal of Criminology* 34: 139–71.

Braithwaite, V. (2004) 'The Hope Process and Social Inclusion', *Annals of the American Academy of Political and Social Science* 592: 128–51.

Brewer, J.D. (1984) 'Competing Understandings of Common-Sense Understanding', *British Journal of Sociology* 35: 66–74.

Brewer, J.D. (1986a) 'Adam Ferguson and the Theme of Exploitation', *British Journal of Sociology* 37: 461–78.

Brewer, J.D. (1986b) *After Soweto*. Oxford: Clarendon Press.

Brewer, J.D. (1988) 'Micro-Sociology and the "Duality of Structure": Former Fascists "Doing" Life History', in N. Fielding (ed.), *Actions and Structure*. London: Sage: 142–66.

Brewer, J.D. (1994) *Black and Blue*. Oxford: Clarendon Press.

Brewer, J.D. (2003) *C. Wright Mills and the Ending of Violence*. London: Palgrave.

Brewer, J.D. (2007) 'Sociology and Theology Reconsidered: Religious Sociology and Sociology of Religion in Britain', *Journal of the History of Human Sciences* 20(2): 7–28.

Brewer, J.D. (2010) *Peace Processes: A Sociological Approach*. Cambridge: Polity Press.

Brewer, J.D. (2013a) *The Public Value of the Social Sciences*. London: Bloomsbury.

Brewer, J.D. (2013b) 'C. Wright Mills on War and Peace', in J. Scott and A. Nilsen (eds), *C. Wright Mills and the Sociological Imagination*. Cheltenham, UK and Northampton, MA, USA: Edward Elgar Publishing: 183–202.

Brewer, J.D. (2013c) 'Sociology and Peacebuilding', in R. Mac Ginty (ed.), *Routledge Handbook of Peacebuilding*. London: Routledge: 159–70.

Brewer, J.D (2014a) 'The Scottish Enlightenment and Scottish Social Thought c.1725–1915', in J. Holmwood and J. Scott (eds), *The Palgrave Handbook of Sociology in Britain*. Basingstoke: Palgrave: 3–29.

Brewer, J.D. (2014b) 'Society as a Vocation: Renewing Social Science for Social Renewal', *Irish Journal of Sociology* 22(2): 127–37.

Brewer, J.D. (2015a) 'Growing up as a Sociologist in Rural Shropshire', in K. Twamley, M. Doidge and A. Scott (eds), *Sociologists' Tales*. Bristol: Policy Press: 71–6.

Brewer, J.D. (2015b) 'Peace Processes', *International Encyclopedia of Social and Behavioral Sciences 2nd Edition*, edited by James Wright, Oxford: Elsevier: 648–53.

Brewer, J.D. (2018a) 'The Sociology of the Northern Irish Peace Process', in C. Armstrong, D. Herbert and J. Mustad (eds), *The Legacy of the Good Friday Agreement*. London: Palgrave: 271–89.

Brewer, J.D. (2018b) 'Conclusion: Afterword on the Sociology of Compromise', in J.D. Brewer, B.C. Hayes and F. Teeney (eds), *The Sociology of Compromise after Conflict*. London: Palgrave: 229–56.

Brewer, J.D. (2018c) 'Towards a Sociology of Compromise' in J.D. Brewer, B.C. Hayes and F. Teeney (eds), *The Sociology of Compromise after Conflict*. London: Palgrave: 1–29.

Brewer, J.D. (2019) 'The Public Value of the Sociology of Religion', in A. Lindgreen, N. Koenig-Lewis, M. Kitchener, J.D. Brewer, M. Moore and T. Meynhardt (eds), *Public Value*. London: Routledge: 222–35.

Brewer, J.D. (2020) 'Remembering Forwards: Healing the Hauntings of the Past', in K. Wale, P. Gobodo-Madikizela and J. Prager (eds), *Post-Conflict Hauntings*. London: Palgrave: 29–46.

Brewer, J.D. (2021a) '"Sin by Silence": The Claims to Moral Legitimacy amongst Northern Irish Paramilitaries', in J.D. Brewer and A. Wahidin (eds), *Ex-Combatant Voices*. London: Palgrave: 93–122.

Brewer, J.D. (2021b) 'Dealing with the Past and Envisioning the Future: Some Problems with Northern Ireland's Peace Process', in L. LeLourec and G. O'Keeffe-Vigneron (eds), *Northern Ireland After the Good Friday Agreement*. Brussels: Peter Lang: 39–56.

Brewer, J.D. (2021c) 'Listening to Ex-Combatants' Voices', in J.D. Brewer and A. Wahidin (eds), *Ex-Combatant Voices*. London: Palgrave: 11–34.

Brewer, J.D. (2021d) 'C. Wright Mills and the Public Sociology of Peace', in J. Frauley (ed.), *The Routledge International Handbook of C. Wright Mills Studies*. Abingdon: Routledge: 115–26.

Brewer, J.D. and Hayes, B.C. (2011a) 'Post-Conflict Societies and the Social Sciences: A Review', *Contemporary Social Science* 6(1): 5–18.

Brewer, J.D. and Hayes, B.C. (2011b) 'Victims as Moral Beacons', *Contemporary Social Science* 6(1): 73–88.

Brewer, J.D. and Hayes, B.C. (2013) 'Victimhood Status and Public Attitudes toward Post-Conflict Agreements: Northern Ireland as a Case Study', *Political Studies* 61: 442–61.

Brewer, J.D. and Hayes, B.C. (2015a) 'Victimisation and Attitudes towards Former Political Prisoners in Northern Ireland', *Terrorism and Political Violence* 27: 741–61.

Brewer, J.D. and Hayes, B.C. (2015b) 'Victimhood and Attitudes towards Dealing with the Legacy of a Violent Past: Northern Ireland as a Case Study', *British Journal of Politics and International Relations* 17(3): 512–30.

REFERENCES 131

Brewer, J.D. and Herron, S. (2021) 'British Counter-Insurgency Veterans in Afghanistan', in J.D. Brewer and A. Wahidin (eds), *Ex-Combatant Voices*. London: Palgrave: 123–48.

Brewer, J.D. and Higgins, G. (1998) *Anti-Catholicism in Northern Ireland 1600–1998*. London: Macmillan.

Brewer, J.D. and Wahidin, A. (eds) (2021) *Ex-Combatant Voices*. London: Palgrave.

Brewer, J.D., Hayes, B.C. and Teeney, F. (eds) (2018) *The Sociology of Compromise after Conflict*. London: Palgrave.

Brewer, J.D., Hayes, B.C., Teeney, F., Dudgeon, K., Mueller-Hirth, N. and Wijesinghe, S.L. (2017) 'Victims as Moral Beacons of Humanitarianism in Post-Conflict Societies', *International Social Science Journal* 65(215/16): 37–48.

Brewer, J.D., Hayes, B.C., Teeney, F., Dudgeon, K., Mueller-Hirth, N. and Wijesinghe, S.L. (2018) *The Sociology of Everyday Life Peacebuilding*. London: Palgrave.

Brewer, J.D., Higgins, G.I. and Teeney, F. (2011) *Religion, Civil Society and the Peace Process in Northern Ireland*. Oxford: Oxford University Press.

Brewer, J.D., Mitchell, D. and Leavey, G. (2013) *Ex-Combatants, Religion and Peace in Northern Ireland*. London: Palgrave.

Brudholm, T. (2008) *Resentment's Virtue*. Philadelphia: Temple University Press.

Brudholm, T. and Cushman, T. (eds) (2009) *The Religious in Response to Mass Atrocity*. Cambridge: Cambridge University Press.

Burawoy, M. (2010) 'Southern Windmill: The Life and Work of Edward Webster', *Transformation* 72/3: 1–25.

Burnett, R. and Maruna, S. (2004) 'So "Prison Works" Does It?', *The Howard Journal of Criminal Justice* 43: 390–404.

Butalia, U. (2000) *The Other Side of Silence*. London: Hurst.

Cadwallader, A. (2013) *Lethal Allies: British Collusion in Ireland*. Blackrock: The Mercier Press.

Calhoun, C. (2000) 'The Virtue of Civility', *Philosophy and Public Affairs* 29: 251–75.

Carberry, E. (2019) 'Transgenerational Trauma'. Unpublished MA Thesis, Senator George J. Mitchell Institute for Global Peace, Security and Justice, Queen's University Belfast.

Caruth, C. (1996) *Unclaimed Experience*. Baltimore: Johns Hopkins University Press.

Chalk, F. and Jonassohn, K. (1990) *The History and Sociology of Genocide*. New Haven: Yale University Press.

Clark, J.N. (2017) 'Masculinity and Male Survivors of Wartime Sexual Violence: A Bosnian Case Study', *Conflict, Security and Development* 17(4): 287–311.

Clark, J.N (2020) 'Finding a Voice: Silence and its Significance for Transitional Justice', *Social & Legal Studies* 29: 355–78.

Coetzee, A. and Du Toit, L. (2018) 'Facing the Sexual Demon of Colonial Power', *European Journal of Women's Studies* 25(2): 214–27.

Connerton, P. (2008) 'Seven Types of Forgetting', *Memory Studies* 1: 59–72.

Coser, L. (1956) *The Social Functions of Conflict*. London: Routledge.

Davies, M. (2010) 'Bauman's Compass: Towards a Sociology of Hope', *Compass* September: 1–8.

Dawe, A. (1970) 'The Two Sociologies', *British Journal of Sociology* 21: 207–18.

Douglas, J., Adler, P.A., Adler, P., Fontana, A., Freeman, C. and Kotarba, J. (1980) *Introduction to the Sociologies of Everyday Life*. London: Allyn and Bacon.

Dzuverovic, N. (2021) '"To Romanticise or not to Romanticise"; Local Agency and Peacebuilding in the Balkans', *Conflict, Security, Development* 21(1): 21–41.

Eastmond, M. and Selimovic, J. (2014) 'Silence as a Possibility in Post-War Everyday Life', *International Journal of Transitional Justice* 6(3): 502–24.

Elias, N. (2000 [1939]) *The Civilizing Process*. Oxford: Wiley-Blackwell.

Elliott, M. (2009) *When God Took Sides*. Oxford: Oxford University Press.

Elster, J. (2004) *Closing the Books*. Cambridge: Cambridge University Press.

Eyerman, R. (2012) 'Cultural Trauma: Emotion and Narration', in J. Alexander, R. Jacobs and P. Smith (eds), *The Oxford Handbook of Cultural Sociology*. Oxford: Oxford University Press. Accessible at https://www.oxfordhandbooks.com/view/10.1093/oxfordhb/9780195377767.001.0001/oxfordhb-9780195377767-e-21.

Felski, R. (1999) 'The Invention of Everyday Life', *New Formations* 39: 15–31.

Fiske, A.P. and Rai, T.S. (2015) *Virtuous Violence*. Cambridge: Cambridge University Press.

Flanagan, K. (1996) *The Enchantment of Sociology*. London: Macmillan.

Frisby, D. and Sayer, D. (1986) *Society*. London: Tavistock Publications.

Galtung, J. (1969) 'Violence, Peace and Peace Research', *Journal of Peace Research* 6: 167–91.

Giddens, A. (1984) *The Constitution of Society*. Cambridge: Polity Press.

Giddens, A. (1990) *The Consequences of Modernity*. Cambridge: Polity Press.

Gilroy, P. (2017) '"Where Every Breeze Speaks of Courage and Liberty"', 2015 *Antipode* RGS-IBG Annual Lecture, published in *Antipode* 50(1): 3–22.

Gobodo-Madikizela, P. (2008) 'Empathetic Repair after Mass Trauma: When Vengeance is Arrested', *European Journal of Social Theory* 11: 331–50.

Gobodo-Madikizela, P. (2012) 'Transitional Justice and Truth Commissions: Exploring Narratives of Repair and Healing in the Post-Holocaust Era', *Psychology, Crime and Law* 18(3): 275–97.

Gobodo-Madikizela, P. (2016a) *What Does it Mean to the Human in the Aftermath of Historical Trauma?* Claude Ake Memorial Paper 9, the Nordic Africa Institute and Uppsala University.

Gobodo-Madikizela, P. (2016b) 'What Does it Mean to be Human in the Aftermath of Mass Trauma and Violence?', *Christian Ethics* 36(2): 43–61.

Gobodo-Madikizela, P. (2020) 'Aesthetics of Memory, Witness to Violence and a Call to Repair', in K. Wale, P. Gobodo-Madikizela and J. Prager (eds), *Post-Conflict Hauntings*. London: Palgrave: 119–49.

Goetze, C. and de Guevara, B. (2021) 'International Political Sociology of Peacebuilding', in O. Richmond and G. Visoka, *The Oxford Handbook of Peacebuilding, Statebuilding and Peace Formation*. Oxford: Oxford University Press: 123–38.

Goffman, E. (1959) *The Presentation of Self in Everyday Life*. London: Penguin.

Goffman, E. (1966) *Behaviour in Public Places*. New York: Simon and Schuster.

Graham, L. (2016) *Beyond Social Capital*. London: Palgrave.

REFERENCES 133

Graham, L. (2018) 'Trust as a Compromise Mediator in Northern Ireland's Victim Support Groups', in J.D. Brewer, B.C. Hayes and F. Teeney (eds), *The Sociology of Compromise after Conflict*. London: Palgrave: 51–74.

Hawthorne, G. (2008) *Enlightenment and Despair* (2nd edn). Cambridge: Cambridge University Press.

Hayes, B.C. and Brewer, J.D. (2018) 'The Road to Compromise in Sri Lanka', in J.D. Brewer, B.C. Hayes and F. Teeney (eds), *The Sociology of Compromise after Conflict*. London: Palgrave: 157–78.

Hayner, P. (2010) *Unspeakable Truths*. Cambridge: Polity Press.

Heelas, P., Lash, S. and Morris, P. (eds) (1995) *Detraditionalization*. Oxford: Blackwell.

Hirsch, D. (2003) *Law against Genocide*. London: Glasshouse.

Hochschild, A. (2003) *The Managed Heart*. Berkeley: University of California Press.

Holmes, M. (2000) 'When is the Personal Political? The President's Penis and Other Stories', *Sociology* 34: 305–21.

Hynes, H.P. (2004) 'On the Battlefield of Women's Bodies', *Women's Studies International Forum* 27: 431–45.

Ignatieff, M. (1998) *The Warrior's Honour*. London: Chatto and Windus.

Ignatieff, M. (2017) *The Ordinary Virtues*. London: Harvard University Press.

Illouz, E. (2007) *Cold Intimacies: The Making of Emotional Capitalism*. Cambridge: Polity Press.

Jankowitz, S. (2018) *The Order of Victimhood*. London: Palgrave.

Jaworski, G.D. (1991) 'The Historical and Contemporary Importance of Coser's Functions', *Sociological Theory* 9(1): 116–23.

Jones, P. (1994) *Rights*. London: Palgrave.

Jones, P. (2013) 'Moral Rights, Human Rights and Social Recognition', *Political Studies* 61(2): 267–81.

Kalberg, S. (1980) 'Max Weber's Types of Rationality', *American Journal of Sociology* 85(5): 1145–79.

Kaldor, M. (1999) *New and Old Wars*. Cambridge: Polity Press.

Kaldor, M. (2013) 'In Defence of New Wars', *Stability* 2(1): 1–16.

Kalekin-Fishman, D. (2013) 'Sociology of Everyday Life', *Current Sociology* 61: 714–32.

Karstedt, S. (2002) 'Emotions and Criminal Justice', *Theoretical Criminology* 6: 299–317.

Kelley, T. (2017) 'Maintaining Power by Manipulating Memory in Rwanda', *Fordham International Law Journal* 41(1): 79–133.

Kelly, G. (2021) 'Reconciliation and Peacebuilding', in O. Richmond and G. Visoka (eds), *The Oxford Handbook of Peacebuilding, Statebuilding and Peace Formation*. Oxford: Oxford University Press: 506–19.

Kimmerling, B. (2012) *Marginal at the Centre*. Brooklyn: Berghahn Books.

King, M.L. Jr (1958) *Stride toward Freedom*. Boston: Beacon Press.

Kingwell, M. (1995) *A Civil Tongue*. Philadelphia: Penn State University Press.

Kovras, I. (2013) 'Explaining Long Silences in Transitional Justice: The Disappeared in Cyprus and Spain', *Comparative Political Studies* 46(6): 730–56.

Kumar, K. and Makarova, E. (2008) 'The Portable Home: The Domestication of Public Space', *Sociological Theory* 26: 324–43.

Kurtz, L.R. and Smithey, L.E. (eds) (2018) *The Paradox of Repression and Non-Violent Movements*. Syracuse: Syracuse University Press.

Langa, M., Maringira, G. and Merafe, M. (2021) 'Contested Voices of Former Combatants in Post-Apartheid South Africa', in J.D. Brewer and A. Wahidin (eds), *Ex-Combatant Voices*. London: Palgrave: 151–78.

Lederach, J.P. (1997) *Building Peace*. Washington, DC: United States Institute for Peace Press.

Lederach, J.P. (1999) 'Justpeace: The Challenge of the 21st century', in Paul van Tongeren (ed.), *In People Building Peace*. Utrecht: European Centre for Conflict Prevention: 27–36.

Lederach, J.P (2005) *The Moral Imagination*. Oxford: Oxford University Press.

Lefebvre, H. (2009) *State, Space, World*. Minneapolis: University of Minnesota Press.

Leonard, M. (2004) 'Bonding and Bridging Social Capital: Reflections from Belfast', *Sociology* 38(5): 927–44.

Leonardsson, H. and Rudd, G. (2015) 'The "Local Turn" in Peacebuilding', *Third World Quarterly* 36(5): 825–39.

Leopora, C. (2012) 'On Compromise and Being Compromised', *Journal of Political Philosophy* 20(1): 1–22.

Leopora, C. and Goodin, R.E. (2013) *On Complicity and Compromise*. Oxford: Oxford University Press.

Lewis, J. and Weigert, A. (1985a) 'Trust as a Social Reality', *Social Forces* 63: 967–85.

Lewis, J. and Weigert, A. (1985b) 'Social Atomism, Holism and Trust', *Sociological Quarterly* 26: 955–71.

Leys, R. (2000) *Trauma: A Genealogy*. Chicago: University of Chicago Press.

Littlewood, R. (1997) 'Military Rape', *Anthropology Today* 13: 7–16.

Loyle, C. and Davenport, C. (2020) 'Some Left to Tell the Tale: Finding Perpetrators and Understanding Violence in Rwanda', *Journal of Peace Research* 57(4): 507–20.

Mac Ginty, R. (2014) 'Everyday Peace: Bottom-Up and Local Agency in Conflict-Afflicted Societies', *Security Dialogue* 45(6): 548–64.

Mac Ginty, R. and Richmond, O. (2013) 'The Local Turn in Peacebuilding', *Third World Quarterly* 34(5): 763–83.

Magadla, S. (2021) 'The Lives of Women Ex-Combatants in Post-Apartheid South Africa', in J.D. Brewer and A. Wahidin (eds), *Ex-Combatant Voices*. London: Palgrave: 179–206.

Malesevic, S. (2010) *The Sociology of War and Violence*. Cambridge: Cambridge University Press.

Margalit, A. (2010) *On Compromise and Rotten Compromises*. Princeton: Princeton University Press.

Marks, S. (1974) 'Durkheim's Theory of Anomie', *American Journal of Sociology* 80(2): 329–63.

McDoom, O.S. (2012) 'The Psychology of Threat in Intergroup Conflict: Emotions, Rationality, and Opportunity in the Rwandan Genocide', *International Security* 37(2): 119–55.

McLaughlin, N. (2021) *Erich Fromm and Global Public Sociology*. Bristol: Bristol University Press.

REFERENCES 135

Meer, F. (2017) *Fatima Meer: Memories of Love and Hope*. Cape Town: Kwela Publishers.

Mihai, M. (2016) *Negative Emotions and Transitional Justice*. New York: Columbia University Press.

Mills, C.W. (1940) 'Situated Actions and Vocabularies of Motive', *American Sociological Review* 5(6): 904–13.

Mills, C.W. (1959a) *The Causes of World War Three*. London: Secker and Warburg.

Mills, C.W. (1959b) *The Sociological Imagination*. Oxford: Oxford University Press.

Misztal, B. (1996) *Trust in Modern Societies*. Cambridge: Polity Press.

Misztal, B. (2003) *Theories of Social Remembering*. Buckingham: Open University Press.

Misztal, B. (2004) 'The Sacralization of Memory', *European Journal of Social Theory* 7(1): 67–84.

Misztal, B. (2011a) *The Challenges of Vulnerability*. London: Palgrave.

Misztal, B. (2011b) 'Forgiveness and the Construction of New Conditions for a Common Life', *Contemporary Social Science* 6(1): 39–53.

Mollering, G. (2001) 'The Nature of Trust', *Sociology* 35: 403–20.

Moses, A.D. (2021) *The Problems of Genocide*. Cambridge: Cambridge University Press.

Motsemme, N. (2004) 'The Mute Always Speak: On Women's Silences in the Truth and Reconciliation Commission', *Current Sociology* 52(5): 909–32.

Moussawi, G. and Vidal-Ortiz, S. (2020) 'A Queer Sociology: On Power, Race and Decentering Whiteness', *Sociological Forum* 35: 1272–89.

Mueller-Hirth, N. (2018) 'Forgiveness and the Practice of Compromise in Post-Apartheid South Africa', in J.D. Brewer, B.C. Hayes and F. Teeney (eds), *The Sociology of Compromise after Conflict*. London: Palgrave: 103–28.

Mun, K., Rojas, H., Coppini, D. and Cho, H. (2021) 'Political Tolerance of Demobilizing Armed Actors: The Case of FARC in Colombia', *Media, War & Conflict* 14(2): 221–38.

Münkler, H. (2005) *The New Wars*. Cambridge: Polity Press.

Murray, A.J. and Durrheim, K. (2021) 'Maintaining the Status Quo Through Repressed Silences', *Sociology* 55(2): 283–99.

Neal, S. and Murji, K. (2015) 'Sociologies of Everyday Life', *Sociology* 49(5): 811–19.

Nichter, B., Norman, S., Maguen, S. and Pietrzak, R. (2021) 'Moral Injury and Suicidal Behavior Amongst US Combat Veterans', *Depression and Anxiety* 38(6): 606–14.

Nisbet, R. (1967) *The Sociological Tradition*. London: Heinemann.

Nisbet, R. (1973) *The Social Philosophers*. New York: Thomas Cromwell Co.

Nussbaum, M. (2001) *Upheavals of Thought*. Cambridge: Cambridge University Press.

Nussbaum, M. (2013) *Political Emotions: Why Love Matters for Justice*. London: Harvard University Press.

Oberschall, A. (2007) *Conflict and Peacebuilding in Divided Societies*. Abingdon: Routledge.

136 ADVANCED INTRODUCTION TO THE SOCIOLOGY OF PEACE PROCESSES

O'Neill, O. (1993) 'Practices of Toleration', in J. Lichtenberg (ed.), *Democracy and the Mass Media*. Cambridge: Cambridge University Press.

Otake, Y. (2019) 'Suffering of Silenced People in Northern Rwanda', *Social Science & Medicine* 222: 171–9.

Paffenhalz, T. (2015) 'Unpacking the Local Turn in Peacebuilding', *Third World Quarterly* 36(5): 857–74.

Paris, R. (2004) *At War's End*. Cambridge: Cambridge University Press.

Petersen, A. and Wilkinson, I. (2015) 'Editorial Introduction: The Sociology of Hope in Contexts of Health, Medicine and Healthcare', *Health* 19(2): 113–18.

Philpott, D. (2012) *Just and Unjust Peace*. Oxford: Oxford University Press.

Pink, S. (2012) *Situating Everyday Life*. London: Sage.

Plummer, K. (2015) *Cosmopolitan Sexualities: Hope and the Humanist Imagination*. Cambridge: Polity Press.

Pollner, M. (1987) *Mundane Reason*. Cambridge: Cambridge University Press.

Prager, J. (2008) 'Healing from History: Psychoanalytic Considerations on Traumatic Pasts and Social Repair', *European Journal of Social Theory* 11: 405–20.

Psathas, G. (1980) 'Approaches to the Study of the World of Everyday Life', *Human Studies* 3(1): 3–17.

Punch, M. (2012) *State Violence, Collusion and the Troubles*. London: Pluto Press.

Putnam, R. (2000) *Bowling Alone*. New York: Simon and Schuster.

Ray, L. (1999) *Theorizing Classical Sociology*. Buckingham: Open University Press.

Ray, L. (2018) *Violence and Society* (2nd edn). London: Sage.

Ray, L., Smith, D. and Wastell, L. (2004) 'Shame, Rage and Racist Violence', *British Journal of Criminology* 44(1): 350–68.

Reid, B. (2008) 'Rearranging the Ground: Public and Private Space in Belfast, Northern Ireland', *Gender, Place and Culture* 15: 489–503.

Rex, J. (1981) *Social Conflict*. London: Longman.

Rieff, D. (2016) *In Praise of Forgetting*. New Haven: Yale University Press.

Runciman, W.G. (1999) *The Social Animal*. London: Fontana.

Scheff, T. (1994) *Bloody Revenge*. Boulder: Westview Press.

Scheff, T. (2000) 'Shame and the Social Bond', *Sociological Theory* 18(1): 84–99.

Scheff, T. (2011a) 'Shame in Self and Society', *Symbolic Interaction* 26(2): 239–67.

Scheff, T. (2011b) 'Alienation, Love and Hate as Causes of Collective Violence', in S. Karstedt, I. Loader and H. Strang (eds), *Emotions, Crime and Justice*. Oxford: Hart: 275–94.

Scheff, T. and Ratzinger, S. (1991) *Emotions and Violence*. Lexington: Lexington Books.

Schwab, G. (2010) *Haunting Legacies: Violent Histories and Transgenerational Trauma*. New York: Columbia University Press.

Scimecca, J. (2019) *Christianity and Sociological Theory*. London: Routledge.

Scott, S. (2009) *Making Sense of Everyday Life*. Cambridge: Polity Press.

Scott, S. (2017) 'A Sociology of Nothing: Understanding the Unmarked', *Sociology* 52(1): 3–19.

Scott, S. (2020) *The Social Life of Nothing*. Abingdon: Routledge.

Seligman, A. (1997) *The Problem of Trust*. Princeton: Princeton University Press.

Seligman, A. (1998) 'Trust and Sociability', *American Journal of Economics and Sociology* 57: 391–404.

REFERENCES 137

Selimovic, J. (2018) 'Gendered Violence in Post-Conflict Societies: A Typology', *Peacebuilding* 8(1): 1–15.

Sen, A. (1999) *Development as Freedom*. New York: Knopf.

Sennett, R. (2003 [1974]) *The Fall of Public Man*. London: Penguin.

Shaw, M. (2005) *The New Western Way of War*. Cambridge: Polity Press.

Shaw, M. (2007) *What is Genocide?* Cambridge: Polity Press.

Shriver, D. (1995) *An Ethic for Enemies: Forgiveness and Politics*. Oxford: Oxford University Press.

Smelser, N. (2004) 'Psychological Trauma and Collective Trauma', in J. Alexander, R. Eyerman, B. Giesen, N. Smelser and P. Sztompka, *Cultural Trauma and Collective Identity*. Berkeley: University of California Press: 31–59.

Smith, Aimee (2018) 'Barriers to Trust in a "Peace Process Generation": Ambivalence in Young Catholics in Northern Ireland', in J.D. Brewer, B.C. Hayes and F. Teeney (eds), *The Sociology of Compromise after Conflict*. London: Palgrave: 75–102.

Smith, Anthony (1976) *Social Change*. London: Longman.

Smith, J. (2021) 'Globalisation of Peace', in O. Richmond and G. Visoka (eds), *The Oxford Handbook of Peacebuilding, Statebuilding and Peace Formation*. Oxford: Oxford University Press: 314–27.

Steen-Johnsen, T. (2020) 'The Rhetoric of Love in Religious Peacebuilding', *Journal of Contemporary Religion* 35(3): 433–48.

Stets, J.E. and Turner, J.H. (eds) (2006) *Handbook of the Sociology of Emotions*. New York: Springer.

Stotland, E. (1969) *The Psychology of Hope*. San Francisco: Jossey-Bass.

Studdart, D. (2016) 'Sociality and a Proposed Analytic for Investigating Communal Being-Ness', *Sociological Review* 64: 622–38.

Sturken, M. (1997) *Tangled Memories*. Berkeley: University of California Press.

Svasek, M. (2005) 'The Politics of Chosen Trauma: Expellee Memories, Emotions and Identities', in K. Milton and M. Svasek (eds), *Mixed Emotions: Anthropological Studies of Feeling*. Oxford: Berg: 195–214.

Sztompka, P. (1999) *Trust: A Sociological Theory*. Cambridge: Cambridge University Press.

Sztompka, P. (2008) 'The Focus on Everyday Life: A New Turn in Sociology', *European Review* 16(1): 23–37.

Tilly, C. (1989) *Big Structures, Large Processes, Huge Comparisons*. New York: Russell Sage Foundation.

Todorov, T. (2003) *Hope and History* (trans. David Bellos). Princeton: Princeton University Press.

Torgovnik, J. (2009) *Intended Consequences: Rwandan Children Born of Rape*. New York: Aperture.

Torrance, A. (2006) *The Theological Grounds for Advocating Forgiveness in the Sociopolitical Realm*. Belfast: Centre for Contemporary Christianity.

Turner, B. (2006) *Vulnerability and Human Rights*. Philadelphia: Pennsylvania State University Press.

Unwin, J. (2016) *A State in Denial*. Cork: The Mercier Press.

Urry, J. (1996) 'How Societies Remember the Past', in S. Macdonald and G. Fyfe (eds), *Theorizing Museums*. Oxford: Blackwell: 45–65.

138 ADVANCED INTRODUCTION TO THE SOCIOLOGY OF PEACE PROCESSES

Verwoerd, W. and Edlmann, T. (2021) '"Why Did I Die?": South African Defence Force Conscripts Pre- and Post-1994', in J.D. Brewer and A. Wahidin (eds), *Ex-Combatant Voices*. London: Palgrave: 207–36.

Volkan, V. (2001) 'Transgenerational Transmissions and Chosen Traumas: An Aspect of Large-Group Identity', *Group Analysis* 34: 79–97.

Walby, S. (1989) 'Theorising Patriarchy', *Sociology* 23(2): 213–34.

Walby, S. (1990) *Theorising Patriarchy*. London: Wiley.

Walby, S. (2013) 'Violence and Society: Introduction to an Emerging Field in Sociology', *Current Sociology* 61(2): 95–111.

Walby, S. (2021) *Theorizing Violence*. Cambridge: Polity Press.

Wale, K., Gobodo-Madikizela, P. and Prager, J. (eds) (2020) *Post-Conflict Hauntings*. London: Palgrave.

Walker, M. (2006) *Moral Repair*. Cambridge: Cambridge University Press.

Wallis, J. (2021) 'The Social Construction of Peace', in O. Richmond and G. Visoka, *The Oxford Handbook of Peacebuilding, Statebuilding and Peace Formation*. Oxford: Oxford University Press: 77–90.

Walsh, D. (1998) 'Structure/Agency', in C. Jenks (ed.), *Core Sociological Dichotomies*. London: Sage: 8–33.

Weber, M. (1968 [1921]) *Economy and Society*, edited by G. Roth and C. Wittich. New York: Bedminster.

Weiss, K. (2010) 'Male Sexual Victimization: Examining Men's Experience of Rape and Sexual Assault', *Men and Masculinities* 12(3): 275–98.

Wijesinghe, S.L. and Brewer, J.D. (2018) 'Peace Religiosity and Forgiveness among War Victims in Sri Lanka', in J.D. Brewer, B.C. Hayes and F. Teeney (eds), *The Sociology of Compromise after Conflict*. London: Palgrave: 129–56.

Wilkinson, I. (2005) *Suffering: A Sociological Introduction*. Cambridge: Polity Press.

Wilkinson, I. and Kleinman, A. (2016) *Risk, Vulnerability and Everyday Life*. Berkeley: University of California Press.

Wilson, Richard (2001) *The Politics of Truth and Reconciliation in South Africa*. Cambridge: Cambridge University Press.

Wolterstorff, N. (2008) *Justice*. Princeton: Princeton University Press.

Wolterstorff, N. (2013) *Journey towards Justice*. Grand Rapids: Baker Academic.

Woods, E.T. (2019) 'Cultural Trauma: Ron Eyerman and the Founding of a New Research Paradigm', *American Journal of Cultural Sociology* 7: 260–74.

Wrong, D. (1961) 'The Oversocialised Conception of Man in Modern Sociology', *American Sociological Review* 26: 184–93.

Wynter, S. (1999) 'The Re-Enchantment of Humanism: An Interview with Sylvia Wynter'. Accessible at https://serendipstudio.org/oneworld/system/files/WynterInterview.pdf.

Index

African National Congress 26, 89, 110
agency vs structure debate in sociology
10-11
Alexander, Jeffrey 100, 102, 103, 104
Also see trauma, sociology of
cultural trauma
anger 17, 20, 43, 44, 55, 58, 60, 61, 63,
80, 81, 91, 99, 113-15, 125
sociology of 42, 64, 65, 66, 67,
68-70, 120, 122
antinomies of peace 24-9, 54
Also see social peace process
Archer, Margaret 17
Arendt, Hannah 51, 57, 63

Beck, Ulrich 18
Also see risk
Bradford University Peace Studies 2
British Sociological Association 17
British sociology 1, 5, 6, 9, 16, 17, 124
Brudholm, Thomas 14, 64, 69

Carberry, Elizabeth 114
cognitivist revolution in sociology 10,
15, 17, 63, 80, 81, 120
collusion 109, 114-16, 117
colonialism, post-colonialism 8, 89,
112, 118
compromise 12, 17, 76, 80, 81, 92, 96,
97, 120, 123, 125
compromise peace processes 23,
31, 33, 34, 35-43, 121, 122,
124, 125-6
sociology of compromise 19,
44-62, 70, 98-9, 121, 122

conflict, sociology of 7-9, 10, 11, 12,
13, 21, 84, 119
Also see order, sociology of

Dawe, Alan 6, 9, 10
disciplinary closure,
inter-disciplinarity 1, 2, 13, 16,
21, 22, 82, 86
Durkheim, Emile 111-12

Elster, Jon 47, 65, 111
emotions 17-18, 43, 45, 63-81, 121, 122
in peace processes 48, 49, 50, 51,
52, 63-81, 121, 122, 125
in transitional justice 57, 58, 63,
64-7, 81
past versus future oriented
emotions 58, 62, 63-4, 67,
68, 78, 80, 81, 87, 92, 95
sociology of emotions 17, 46,
47-8, 63
Also see anger, compromise,
forgiveness, guilt, hope,
mercy, shame, trust
Enlightenment 5
in Scotland 5, 16, 124
everyday life 8, 10, 13, 24, 25, 72, 83-5,
122, 125
everyday life peacebuilding, sociology
of 1, 25, 43, 82-99, 122
and mundane reasoning 86-98,
104
ex-combatants 13, 38, 40, 43, 64, 65,
81, 110, 111, 121
Also see martyr-hero-demon
syndrome

139

Ferguson, Adam 5, 11
forgiveness 17, 20, 29, 35, 36, 43, 45, 50, 51, 52, 53, 54, 57, 59, 61, 63, 64, 65, 67, 68, 74, 93, 94, 95, 99, 122, 125
  sociology of forgiveness 42, 70-3, 80, 81
  versus forgetting 51, 61, 74, 94, 125

Galtung, Johan 2, 12, 24, 25, 54
gendered violence 9, 13, 14, 102, 106, 118
  and silencing 106, 108, 109, 112
genocide 13, 14, 41, 109
Giddens, Anthony 11, 74
globalisation 7, 18, 19, 120
Gobodo-Madikizela, Pumla 57, 64, 94, 101
Goffman, Erving 48, 49, 83, 97
guilt 43, 58, 63, 65, 66, 67, 78, 80, 102, 113

Hawthorne, Geoffrey 6
hidden victims 104, 105, 106, 107, 109, 110, 111, 112, 113, 114, 117, 118
  and collusion in Northern Ireland 114-16, 117
  and gender 106, 108, 109, 112
  and moral duty 117-18
Holocaust 14, 41, 63, 103, 104, 105
Holocaust model of victimhood 57, 58, 61, 63, 64
hope 17, 19, 20, 39, 42, 43, 54, 55, 61, 63, 64, 67, 68, 92, 122, 125
  sociology of hope 50-1, 78-9, 81

Ignatieff, Michael 13, 46

Kaldor, Mary 15
  Also see new wars
King, Martin Luther Jr 26

Lederach, John Paul 3, 26, 30, 37, 67
legacy issues in peace processes 31, 36, 37, 57, 63, 64, 66, 67, 73, 80, 122, 126

and moral recalibration 39-41
Leverhulme Trust study of victims 62, 65, 76, 87, 98

Mac Ginty, Roger 85, 86, 98
Mandela, Nelson 91, 94, 127
Margalit, Avishai 17, 50
martyr-hero-demon syndrome 40-1, 43, 121
  Also see ex-combatants
Meer, Fatima 3
memory 21, 35, 36, 37-8, 40, 43, 51, 61, 72, 73, 101, 102, 104, 109, 111, 117, 118, 122, 125, 126
  pathological memory cultures 37-8, 43, 126
  Also see remembering forwards
mercy 36, 43, 61, 63, 64, 68, 80, 81, 122, 125
  sociology of mercy 73-4
Mills, C Wright 16, 17, 46, 52, 105, 118
  Also see sociological imagination
Misztal, Barbara 17
moral sensibility 16, 17, 18, 27, 35, 37, 41, 42, 43, 44, 45, 46, 48, 55, 58, 60, 61, 64, 66, 69, 70, 77, 79, 80, 81, 82, 86, 89, 95, 98, 99, 121, 122-6
  and peace 18, 21, 35, 37, 43, 44, 46, 55, 58, 59, 60, 61, 82
  and shared society 126-7
  and sociability, relational ethic of 45, 56, 58, 59, 60, 61, 82, 95, 98, 125
  and sociology of peace processes 18-21, 29, 38, 55-60, 64, 121
mundane reasoning 82, 84, 85, 91, 93, 95, 96-9
  Also see everyday life, everyday life peacebuilding

new wars 4, 15, 19, 124
  and moral injuries 15
Nisbet, Robert 5, 6

INDEX 141

Northern Ireland 12, 27, 28, 29, 42, 52, 56, 59, 62, 65, 76, 77, 85, 86, 87, 88, 90, 93, 95, 110, 111, 114-16, 117
   and Good Friday Agreement 27, 66
Nussbaum, Martha 17, 48

Oberschall, Anthony 3
order, sociology of 4-7, 10, 11, 12, 13, 21, 84, 119
   Also see conflict, sociology of

peace, sociological definition of 29-30, 43, 45, 121, 124
   peace and moral sensibility 18, 21, 35, 37, 43, 44, 46, 55, 58, 59, 60, 61, 82
peace process, sociological definition of 30
   sociological typology of peace processes 31-5
   Also see compromise peace processes
Pollner, Melvin 84, 97
   Also see mundane reasoning
Prutton, Kisane 22
public-private distinction in sociology 19, 41, 47
   in the sociology of compromise 42, 22, 46, 48-50, 56
public sociology 123
public value of the social sciences 122-3

reconciliation 120-1
re-enchantment of the social sciences 15-21, 57, 63, 120, 122, 124
   and moral sensibility 15, 18-19, 20, 21
   political economy of 4, 18-21, 43, 61, 63, 120
religious peacebuilding 3, 43
remembering forwards 43, 94
Rex, John 9, 34
risk 17, 18, 19, 75, 86
Rodgers, Paul 3

Runciman, Walter, 3rd Viscount of Doxford 12 [editor, this is Doxford, not Oxford]
Rwanda 12, 14, 106, 109, 110

Scott, Susie 85, 106, 108
shame 17, 19, 58, 63, 64, 65, 66, 78, 80, 81, 102, 103, 112, 113
silence, silencing 101, 105, 106-10, 112, 113, 114, 117, 118
   and gender 106, 108, 109, 112
Smith, Anthony 8
social justice, injustice 12, 18, 25, 26, 29, 43, 93
   and peace 29, 30, 54, 55, 59 119, 121, 123, 124, 125
social peace process 23, 24, 28, 29, 30, 34, 35, 38, 40, 42, 43, 45, 56, 60, 64, 74, 80, 81
sociological imagination 1, 2, 30, 52, 54, 66, 82, 105, 118
sociology
   of anger *see* anger, sociology of
   of compromise *see* compromise, sociology of
   of conflict *see* conflict, sociology of
   of emotions *see* emotions, sociology of
   of everyday life peacebuilding *see* everyday life peacebuilding, sociology of
   of forgiveness *see* forgiveness, sociology of
   of hope *see* hope, sociology of
   of mercy *see* mercy, sociology of
   of order *see* order, sociology of
   of suffering *see* suffering, sociology of
   of trauma *see* trauma, sociology of cultural trauma, sociology of personal trauma
   of trust *see* trust, sociology of
   of violence *see* violence, sociology of
   of vulnerability *see* vulnerability, sociology of
   of war *see* war, sociology of

142 ADVANCED INTRODUCTION TO THE SOCIOLOGY OF PEACE PROCESSES

South Africa 3, 9, 26, 27, 32, 42, 52, 55, 57, 59, 62, 76, 82, 89, 91, 93, 94, 96, 97, 105, 108, 110, 113, 117, 127
Sri Lanka 28, 33, 42, 52, 53, 55, 59, 62, 76, 82, 86, 87, 89, 91, 92, 94, 95, 105, 110, 117
suffering, sociology of 3

transitional justice 3, 23, 47, 58, 62, 63, 64-7, 78, 80, 81, 106
trauma 3, 45, 58, 65
and chosen trauma 102-3
and inter-generational trauma 60, 101, 105, 106, 108, 113, 114, 117, 118
and post-traumatic stress disorder 42, 58
and sociology of cultural trauma 43, 65, 101-5
and sociology of personal trauma 100, 101, 106-22
trust 27, 50, 52, 61, 64, 68, 70, 73, 91, 123, 125
sociology of trust 74-7, 78, 81, 99, 122
truth recovery 101, 106, 117
Turner, Bryan 17

Walby, Sylvia 13, 14
Also see violence, sociology of
war, sociology of 4, 8, 13, 15, 120
Also see new wars
Weber, Max 16, 87
Webster, Eddie 3
Wolterstorff, Nicholas 17, 50
Woodhouse, Tom 2

United States of America 1, 7, 9, 11, 16, 17, 70, 83, 113

victimhood 33, 41, 42, 44, 53, 56, 57, 58, 59, 60, 61, 63, 65, 66, 69, 70, 86, 87, 88-90, 92, 94, 95, 98, 101, 109, 110, 111, 112, 114, 118, 121
and sociability 57-61, 64, 95-8
double victimhood 53, 89
Holocaust model of 57, 58, 61, 63, 64
social construction of 41-2, 111
Also see hidden victims
violence, sociology of 4, 13-15, 18, 19, 120
virtuous violence 14, 63
vulnerability, sociology of 3, 17, 19, 45

Titles in the Elgar Advanced Introductions series include:

International Political Economy
Benjamin J. Cohen

The Austrian School of Economics
Randall G. Holcombe

Cultural Economics
Ruth Towse

Law and Development
Michael J. Trebilcock and Mariana Mota Prado

International Humanitarian Law
Robert Kolb

International Trade Law
Michael J. Trebilcock

Post Keynesian Economics
J.E. King

International Intellectual Property
Susy Frankel and Daniel J. Gervais

Public Management and Administration
Christopher Pollitt

Organised Crime
Leslie Holmes

Nationalism
Liah Greenfeld

Social Policy
Daniel Béland and Rianne Mahon

Globalisation
Jonathan Michie

Entrepreneurial Finance
Hans Landström

International Conflict and Security Law
Nigel D. White

Comparative Constitutional Law
Mark Tushnet

International Human Rights Law
Dinah L. Shelton

Entrepreneurship
Robert D. Hisrich

International Tax Law
Reuven S. Avi-Yonah

Public Policy
B. Guy Peters

The Law of International Organizations
Jan Klabbers

International Environmental Law
Ellen Hey

International Sales Law
Clayton P. Gillette

Corporate Venturing
Robert D. Hisrich

Public Choice
Randall G. Holcombe

Private Law
Jan M. Smits

Consumer Behavior Analysis
Gordon Foxall

Behavioral Economics
John F. Tomer

Cost–Benefit Analysis
Robert J. Brent

Environmental Impact Assessment
Angus Morrison Saunders

Comparative Constitutional Law
Second Edition
Mark Tushnet

National Innovation Systems
Cristina Chaminade, Bengt-Åke Lundvall and Shagufta Haneef

Ecological Economics
Matthias Ruth

Private International Law and Procedure
Peter Hay

Freedom of Expression
Mark Tushnet

Law and Globalisation
Jaakko Husa

Regional Innovation Systems
Bjørn T. Asheim, Arne Isaksen and Michaela Trippl

International Political Economy
Second Edition
Benjamin J. Cohen

International Tax Law
Second Edition
Reuven S. Avi-Yonah

Social Innovation
Frank Moulaert and Diana MacCallum

The Creative City
Charles Landry

European Union Law
Jacques Ziller

Planning Theory
Robert A. Beauregard

Tourism Destination Management
Chris Ryan

International Investment Law
August Reinisch

Sustainable Tourism
David Weaver

Austrian School of Economics
Second Edition
Randall G. Holcombe

U.S. Criminal Procedure
Christopher Slobogin

Platform Economics
Robin Mansell and W. Edward Steinmueller

Public Finance
Vito Tanzi

Feminist Economics
Joyce P. Jacobsen

Human Dignity and Law
James R. May and Erin Daly

Space Law
Frans G. von der Dunk

National Accounting
John M. Hartwick

Legal Research Methods
Ernst Hirsch Ballin

Privacy Law
Megan Richardson

International Human Rights Law
Second Edition
Dinah L. Shelton

Law and Artificial Intelligence
*Woodrow Barfield and
Ugo Pagello*

Politics of International
Human Rights
David P. Forsythe

Community-based Conservation
Fikret Berkes

Global Production Networks
Neil M. Coe

Mental Health Law
Michael L. Perlin

Law and Literature
Peter Goodrich

Creative Industries
John Hartley

Global Administration Law
Sabino Cassese

Housing Studies
William A.V. Clark

Global Sports Law
Stephen F. Ross

Public Policy
B. Guy Peters

Empirical Legal Research
Herbert M. Kritzer

Cities
Peter J. Taylor

Law and Entrepreneurship
Shubha Ghosh

Mobilities
Mimi Sheller

Technology Policy
*Albert N. Link and James A.
Cunningham*

Urban Transport Planning
Kevin J. Krizek and David A. King

Legal Reasoning
*Larry Alexander and Emily
Sherwin*

Sustainable Competitive
Advantage in Sales
Lawrence B. Chonko

Law and Development
Second Edition
*Mariana Mota Prado and Michael
J. Trebilcock*

Law and Renewable Energy
Joel B. Eisen

Experience Economy
Jon Sundbo

Marxism and Human Geography
Kevin R. Cox

Maritime Law
Paul Todd

American Foreign Policy
Loch K. Johnson

Water Politics
Ken Conca

Business Ethics
John Hooker

Employee Engagement
Alan M. Saks and Jamie A. Gruman

Governance
Jon Pierre and B. Guy Peters

Demography
Wolfgang Lutz

Environmental Compliance and Enforcement
LeRoy C. Paddock

Migration Studies
Ronald Skeldon

Landmark Criminal Cases
George P. Fletcher

Comparative Legal Methods
Pier Giuseppe Monateri

U.S. Environmental Law
E. Donald Elliott and Daniel C. Esty

Gentrification
Chris Hamnett

Family Policy
Chiara Saraceno

Law and Psychology
Tom R. Tyler

Advertising
Patrick De Pelsmacker

New Institutional Economics
Claude Ménard and Mary M. Shirley

The Sociology of Sport
Eric Anderson and Rory Magrath

The Sociology of Peace Processes
John D. Brewer